THE THINKING THINGS

HTTP://WWW.THETHINKINGTHINGS.COM

ALSO BY JOSEPH PALLY

FAIL FAST, MOVE FASTER

HTTP://WWW.FAILFASTMOVEFASTER.COM

THE THINKING THINGS

Web 3.0 *AND BEYOND…*

THE STORY OF THE EVOLUTION TO THE
SEMANTIC OMNI-FUNCTIONAL WEB

BY

JOSEPH PALLY

SILKRAYS PUBLISHING, TEXAS

UNITED STATES

The Thinking Things
Web 3.0 and beyond...
The Story of the Evolution to the Semantic Omni-functional Web

http://www.TheThinkingThings.com

Copyright © 2009 by Joseph Pally

Illustrations by:
Aneesh, Das, Deepu, Jay, Karnan, Mahesh, Prasanth and Varun.

Silkrays books may be ordered through booksellers or by contacting:

Silkrays Publishing Corporation
www.silkrays.com
silkrays.publishing@gmail.com

Based on true historical events.
Web addresses and links in the book may change or may no longer be valid. References are available at the website http://www.TheThinkingThings.com.

ISBN: 978-0-9824326-2-4 (pbk)

Printed in the United States of America.
Silkrays Rev. Date: 04/01/2009

Dedicated to:

SIR TIMOTHY BERNERS-LEE
OM, KBE, FRS, FRENG, FRSA

THE HUMBLE INVENTOR

"The best way to predict the future is to invent it."
Alan Kay
(Computer Scientist, b. 1940)

******

"A tool is but the extension of a man's hand, and a machine is but a complex tool. And he that invents a machine augments the power of a man and the well-being of mankind."
Henry Ward Beecher
(Social Reformer and Speaker, 1813–1887)

******

"Discovery consists of seeing what everybody has seen and thinking what nobody else has thought."
Jonathan Swift
(Author, 1667–1745)

******

"There's nobody getting rich writing software that I know of."
Bill Gates
(CEO, Philanthropist, b. 1955)

******

"Difficult to see. Always in motion is the future."
Yoda
(Jedi Master, 896 BBY–4ABY)

******

CONTENTS

ONLY BARBARIANS ARE NOT CURIOUS ABOUT
WHERE THEY COME FROM,
HOW THEY CAME TO BE WHERE THEY ARE,
WHERE THEY APPEAR TO BE GOING,
WHETHER THEY WISH TO GO THERE,
AND IF SO, WHY, AND IF NOT, WHY NOT.

SIR ISAIAH BERLIN

CHAPTER 1
THE MECHANISM

A century ago, six divers were heading to their hometown of Syme, Greece. Their voyage bordered the Ionian and the Aegean seas – the northern arms of Mediterranean Sea. The usually deep blue calm had given way to heavy weather. They chose to take shelter on a small island nearby.

They were sponge divers by trade. When the storm subsided, Captain Dimitrios sent a few of the divers to check out the seafloor.

The first diver, Elias, was filled with fear as he burst out of the water. He had seen dead people, still horses and pale women – this seafloor was haunted, he was sure.

Dimitrios decided to take a look. After a deep dive, he came back with a bronze arm. At a depth of 140 feet from the surface, the divers had unearthed a long lost Roman ship full of Greek treasures, possibly looted. The wreck had occurred *two thousand* years ago.

The Greek Government heard about the discovery. They arranged to send divers out to the submerged site to bring back more of the ancient artifacts. The first undersea archaeological investigation was on. The dives continued for many years – until one diver died from the bends (decompression sickness) and two were paralyzed.

The treasures that the divers retrieved from the wreckage were truly astonishing.

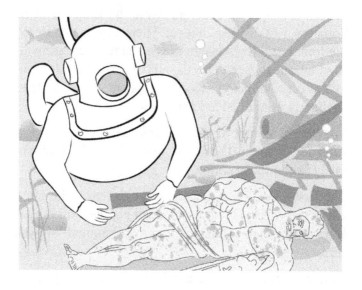

A bronze statue by the Greek sculptor Lysippus.

A statue of haunting grace, the Ephebe, possibly representing Paris, the King of Troy.

And many more, from thousands of years ago.

Yet it was what archaeologist Valerios Stais found on the 17 May 1902 that eclipsed everything else.

During his dive, he had noticed a gear-wheel-like contraption embedded in a piece of rock.

It would take almost a century to understand this strange device. At first, many thought it was some type of clockwork. In 1998, X-ray tomography revealed intricate details about this complex device. By 2006, more research exposed about two thousand characters of text that were etched into the surface of the device. The secrets of the machine were being unearthed a letter at a time. Each gear tooth in this machine had some meaning.

The contraption was called the *Antikythera Mechanism*. The machine could calculate the positions of the Sun, the Moon and the planets – Mercury, Venus, Mars, Jupiter and Saturn. It could predict eclipses and track the four year cycle of the Ancient Olympics.

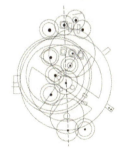 

3

This complex device of differential gears and connectors, developed a hundred years before Jesus Christ, was possibly one of the first analog computing devices. Its discovery caused a paradigm shift – devices of such complexity had not been known to exist until the 1800s.

Babylonian astronomical calculations and techniques from 250 BC were known to the Greeks. But no one expected the ancient Greeks to construct a *computing device* that could implement these complex calculations. That pointed to a completely unexpected level of technological sophistication – that predated Julius Ceaser, the Roman Dictator.

The human search to automate thought and computation had started possibly a century before Christianity itself!

******

CHAPTER 2
THE LARGEST NUMBER

It was a nine year old boy, Milton Sirotta, who named 10^{100} a *Googol*. His uncle Edward Kasner, a mathematician, popularized Googol in his book *Mathematics and the Imagination*, published in 1940.

A Googol is the huge number: 10,000,000,000,000, 000,000,000,000,000,000,000,000,000,000,000, 000,000,000,000,000,000,000,000,000,000,000, 000,000,000,000,000.

The total number of atoms in the entire universe count to approximately 10^{80}, which is less than a Googol! Now you know how big a Googol is.

******

A Googol is also approximately equal to 70! (70 *factorial*=1x2x3x4x...x69x70). That means there are a Googol ways to arrange 70 different things in a sequence.

It is interesting to note that the number of ways to arrange just 70 items in a sequence is greater than the number of atoms in the entire universe.

******

ORDERS OF MAGNITUDE

10^9 — NUMBER OF SECONDS IN 100 YEARS

10^{12} — US FEDERAL DEBT ($)

10^{17} — NUMBER OF SECONDS SINCE BIG BANG

10^{19} — NUMBER OF POSITIONS IN A RUBIK'S CUBE

10^{21} — NUMBER OF SAND GRAINS ON EARTH

10^{22} — NUMBER OF STARS IN VISIBLE UNIVERSE

10^{28} — NUMBER OF ATOMS IN A HUMAN BODY

10^{30} — MASS OF THE SUN (KG)

10^{40} — NUMBER OF CHESS POSITIONS

10^{67} — NUMBER OF COMBINATIONS OF 52 CARDS

10^{80} — NUMBER OF PHYSICAL PARTICLES IN THE UNIVERSE

10^{100} — Googol — GOOGOL

10^{768} — NUMBER OF POSITIONS IN GO (2500 YEARS OLD CHINESE GAME)

The same nine year old boy, Milton, took Googol to the next logical level. He proposed a Googolplex as 10^{googol}.

In the popular TV series *Cosmos*, Carl Sagan suggested that the number Googolplex, if attempted to be written in the decimal system would need more space than *the entire observable universe*. Amazing!

******

CHAPTER 3
AND THE BUDDHA SAID…

Large numbers were not that useful thousands of years ago, but were of intellectual interest to the inquisitive.

In *Lalitavitsara*, a religious book from two thousand years ago written by Bodhisattva, Lord Buddha was quoted listing a series of mega numbers unheard of at that time. These numbers ranged from *koti* (10^7) to *dhvajagranishamani* (10^{421}).

There are also claims that a number like $10^{37218383881977644441306597687849648128}$ has been mentioned in the Buddhist work *Avatamsaka Sutra*.

In today's world, this may look mystifying, but it shows that even two millennia ago, the human mind fancied such large numbers.

******

Next, let us meet Archimedes, another curious mind and a true visionary, who loved large numbers.

******

Koti — 10^7

Ayuta — 10^9

Niyuta — 10^{11}

Kankara — 10^{13}

Vivara — 10^{15}

Akshobhya — 10^{17}

Vivaha — 10^{19}

Utsanga — 10^{21}

Bahula — 10^{23}

Nagabala — 10^{25}

Titlambha — 10^{29}

Vyavasthanapajnapati — 10^{31}

Hetuhila — 10^{33}

Karahu — 10^{35}

Hetvindriya — 10^{37}

Samaptalambha — 10^{39}

Gananagati — 10^{41}

Niravadya — 10^{43}

Mudrabala — 10^{45}

Sarvabala — 10^{47}

Visamjnagatis — 10^{49}

Sarvajna — 10^{51}

Vibhutangama — 10^{53}

Abbuda — 10^{56}

Nirabbuda — 10^{63}

Ahaha — 10^{70}

Ababa — 10^{77}

Atata — 10^{84}

Soganghika — 10^{91}

Uppala — 10^{98}

Kumuda — 10^{105}

Pundarika — 10^{112}

Paduma — 10^{119}

Kathana — 10^{126}

Mahakathana — 10^{133}

Asankheya — 10^{140}

Dhvajagranishamani — 10^{421}

CHAPTER 4
COUNTING EVERY PARTICLE

Cicero once described Syracuse, Sicily, as the greatest Greek city and the most beautiful of them all!

While strolling on the beaches of Syracuse, Archimedes felt a strange desire to count all the grains of sand in the entire Universe.

At a time when the rest of Greece stopped counting at a myriad (10,000), Archimedes took numbers literally to a truly exponential level.

To count all the sand particles in the universe, he devised a numbering scheme with a base of myriad-myriad (10^8, or a hundred million).

The largest number in his numbering system was $10^{80,000,000,000,000,000}$, which is one followed by roughly *eighty–thousand-million-million zeroes* or 80 quadrillion zeroes. He called this huge number '*myriakis-myriostas periodu myriakis-myriston arithmon myriai myriades*'.

In his calculations, he used a heliocentric model for the solar system; but used an incorrect diameter for the entire universe.

With those assumptions, he estimated that there are approximately 10^{64} sand particles in the entire universe.

That still compares well against today's estimate of 10^{80} particles in the entire universe.

******

CHAPTER 5
ABSURD NUMBERS

Were the numbers mentioned by Buddha or Archimedes the largest numbers that we could imagine? Not so, it appears!

Enter some computer scientists and a problem called 'busy beavers'. Busy Beaver is a special case scenario of a *Turing Machine*, which is a machine that is useful only to theoreticians.

Let us find out what such a machine looks like.

TURING MACHINE

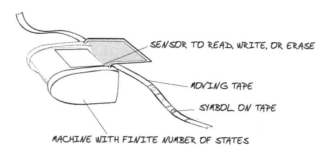

SENSOR TO READ, WRITE, OR ERASE

MOVING TAPE

SYMBOL ON TAPE

MACHINE WITH FINITE NUMBER OF STATES

In computer science, a Turing Machine is a 'theoretical' or imaginary machine similar to a tape recorder. Such imaginary machines are used by computer scientists to argue and theorize about mathematical problems.

The Turing Machine has a head that reads from (and writes to) a long tape. This machine can read and write only a finite set of letters (or alphabet). While accessing the tape, the head of the Turing Machine may move left or right in steps, based on certain rules.

For an alphabet of just 6 letters, the number of steps in the Busy Beaver problem expands to numbers as high as 10^{1400}.

Beyond that, it starts to explode as we will see a bit later. But before we go any further into even larger numbers, we need to learn about a new arithmetic operation called *tetration*.

Tetration

$$^{4}2 = 2^{\left(2^{\left(2^{(2)}\right)}\right)} = 2^{\left(2^{(4)}\right)} = 2^{(16)} = 65536$$

Exponentiation

$$2^{2^{2^{2}}} = (2)^{2*2*2} = 2^{8} = 256$$

As in the figure, tetration looks like exponentiation, but is very different. Exponentiation of 2 four times equals 256, since the exponents are multiplied. On the other hand, tetration of $^{4}2$ zooms to a much larger 2^{16} which equals 65536.

In tetration, the 'tetrated exponents' are expanded first from *top to bottom*, rather than simply multiplied as in exponentiation.

Tetration gets astounding. A simple $^{3}3$ equals 7,625,597,484,987. And a simpler looking $^{4}4$ has more than a 10^{154} digits. That is more than googol digits!

******

In the Busy Beaver scenario mentioned earlier, for an alphabet of 12, the number of steps explodes to a hyper-astronomical $^{166}4096$.

Let us try to grasp this. For an alphabet of 12, the number of Busy Beaver steps may become 4096 tetrated to 4096 itself from top exponent down, 166 times! An absurd number!

******

As if that is not amazing, scientists have devised numbers like Skewes' Number, Moser's Number and Graham's Number.

The latter, Graham's Number, has been the largest number ever used in mathematical proofs. It is so large and complex that it cannot even be expressed easily on paper. Conceptually, it consists of 64 layers of intricately tetrated terms. Graham's number, scientists say, due to theoretical reasons will have …27262464195387 as the last few digits.

Other than that, it will blow your mind!

I'll tell you why. But before that, let's look at a great mind named Max Planck.

******

CHAPTER 6
THE GOD'S UNITS

"In physics, almost everything is already discovered, and all that remains is to fill a few unimportant holes," said Philipp von Jolly, a professor at the University of Munich, to a twenty-year-old Max Planck.

Planck never really wished to discover new things; he just wanted to understand physics at the most fundamental level. In spite of the warning from his professor, Planck switched to studying theoretical physics in 1877.

After a decade, he was commissioned by electric companies to find better ways of reducing energy consumption. This involved working with a device called the 'incandescent electric light bulb' that had recently been invented by a young man named Thomas Alva Edison. While toying with the idea of black body radiation, Planck came out with the equation $E=h\nu$, which gave the energy of an electromagnetic radiation as the product of a constant h (Planck's constant) and ν (the frequency of the wave).

This was the beginning of quantum physics. What the young Max Planck had launched, was a totally new and fundamental branch of physics!

******

The Planck's constant eventually helped him to formulate a new fundamental set of units based only on physical constants (such as the gravitational constant, (G), the speed of light in vacuum (c), the Coulomb force constant (k_e), and the Boltzman's constant (k_B)). Some call Planck's fundamental units as *God's Units*, because they are not dependent on anything created by man.

Let us first consider the God's unit of length: the Planck Length (or p. l. for short). It is so small, that a *single proton* is about a *hundred billion billion* Planck Lengths wide.

That is, a proton is about 10^{20} p. l. wide.

The time interval for light to travel this really tiny distance of 1 p. l. is defined as 1 Planck Time unit (or 1 p. t.). It is so short that nothing noticeable happens in time intervals smaller than this.

Now let us imagine a miniscule cube of one Planck Length on each side.

Let us call this absurdly tiny cube one Planck Volume (1 p. v.).

A Planck Volume is possibly the *smallest* thing you can imagine!

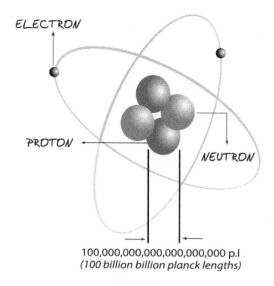

100,000,000,000,000,000,000 p.l
(100 billion billion planck lengths)

******

Now let us shift our attention to the largest thing we can conceptualize. For that, let us take a look at light itself.

Light travels at 300,000 kilometers/second (186,000 miles per second). A ray of light travels so fast that it will circle the earth *eight times in one second.*

A *light year* is the distance a ray of light would travel, if it traveled non-stop for a whole year. Hence, a light year is about *10 trillion kilometers* (or about *6 trillion miles*).

******

The entire observable universe is about *100 billion light years* wide. In fact, our universe is so vast that we cannot even see the light from its edges for another tens-of-billions of years!

<<<------------100,000,000,000 light years--------------->>>
(100 Billion LY)

******

Now we have the Planck Volume, which is the *smallest* physical dimension we can imagine. And the entire observable universe, which is the *largest* physical concept we can imagine.

Let us revisit the Graham's number from the last chapter, by comparing the smallest and the largest things we can think about.

Graham's number consists of 64 layers of recursively tetrated terms, one built over the other like in a tree. Let us take just the very first of these sixty-four layers of terms for comparison.

Even this number that is at the lowest level of Graham's number, is larger than the count of *all of the cubes of Planck Volumes size in the entire observable universe.*

Maybe now you can possibly imagine the huoooooooooooooooooooomongous-ness of Graham's number.

The bottom line is that such numbers are far bigger than our entire universe. It is truly *incomprehensible*!

******

That has not stopped mathematicians from devising yet bigger and absurd numbers such as TREE(n), which makes Graham's Number insignificant for just n=3. TREE(3) is far greater than Graham's number itself. Now think of TREE(1,000,000) or even worse *TREE(googolplex)*!

We routinely underestimate the concept of infinity itself. In a way, numbers can far exceed our imagination so much that 'mind-blowing' may not just be an expression!

******

Clearly, these larger and larger numbers that scientists may come up with will eclipse everything that we know about, and may even care to know about.

However, from the smallest to the largest it matters how we *represent* numbers, to be able to use them for any practical purpose.

That brings us to back to the reality of numbers and numbering systems in the evolution of human thought.

The race to represent numbers and logic would eventually culminate in a revolution called the computer – a thinking thing. But how did the numbering systems evolve? That is next.

******

CHAPTER 7
THE MYRIAD OF NUMBERING SYSTEMS

Archeological records suggest that collections of rocks and bones, carvings and ropes with knots have been used to count and record numbers since 50,000 years ago.

Examples include the Ishango Bone and the Lebombo Bone from Africa, which may have been used to track lunar cycles or other rhythmic events in nature using tally marks.

Tallying sticks could be considered to be the earliest memory device used by humans, to count and store numbers.

Similar techniques were also used in the *Census Quipu* of the Andes, which is a set of strings with knots in each string, to indicate several threads of counting.

******

Even to the earliest mathematicians, 60 was always an interesting number.

60 has twelve factors: 1, 2, 3, 4, 5, 6, 10, 12, 15, 20, 30 and 60. Factors make fractions easier. It is also the smallest number divisible by 1, 2, 3, 4, 5 and 6.

This is possibly why 4500 years ago, Sumerians picked a sexagesimal numbering system to count, which is based on 60.

We still depend on the Sumerian numbering system to measure angles and time.

A full circle has 360 degrees in angle, where each degree is divided into 60 minutes, and each minute is divided into 60 seconds.

We measure time in hours, where each hour is divided into 60 minutes and each minute is divided into 60 seconds.

All thanks to the Sumerians, from four millennia ago!

23

******

We may assume that the decimal system is the most natural for humans, since we have 10 fingers or toes. However, many cultures took stabs at a variety of numbering systems, not all based on the number 10.

For example, the Yuki people of Northern California counted based on spaces between their fingers, rather than the fingers themselves. Hence they ended up with a quaternary (4-based) counting system.

The Maya people of the Americas used a vigesimal numeral system (20-based). Maybe they counted using all fingers on their hands and feet.

The unique footwear worn by the Mayans had openings for toes, which may have been a factor in the perpetuation of this system.

For the Mayan people, one was written as a dot, five with a bar and zero with a shell-shape.

For example, let us add 7 to 2 using the Mayan System, as in the following figure. Seven is written with one bar and two dots on top. Two is written with two dots.

So to add seven and two, the answer nine can be obtained by placing two more dots next to the two existing dots over the seven, resulting in four dots and a dash (which equals nine). Anytime, five dots came together, it is made into a bar.

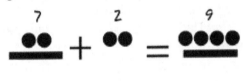

******

Numbering systems and their representations had a significant impact on how far humans *could think* using them. Human effectiveness with numbers and logic was constrained by the complexities of the representations for thousands of years.

Then, half-a-world away, a new numbering system appeared about 1500 years ago that changed everything.

******

CHAPTER 8
HINDUS AND MUSLIMS

The Indian Numeral System with decimal numbers, negative numbers and the concept of zero came into existence around 500 AD.

The Indian Decimal System was enhanced and codified three hundred years later by an Arab, *Muhammad ibn Musa al-Khwarizmi*. His last name *al-Khwarizmi* (later Latinized to *Algoritmi*) gave birth to the word *algorithm (or algorism)* – which today means any technique that is used to describe a computational procedure.

Khwarizmi's book *The Compendious Book on Calculation by Completion and Balancing* (820 AD) explained how to express equations and find solutions to unknown variables by two operations:
Completion (*al gabr*) and Balancing (*al muqabala*).

Completion transfers a negative quantity from one side of an equation to the other as a positive quantity. For example, a – b = c can be converted to a = c + b.

26

The Arabic term *al gabr* (for completion) eventually evolved into the term *algebra*.

Balancing adds the same quantity to both sides of an equation. For example, a + c = b + c can be converted to a = b, by removing c from both sides.

The Arabic term *al muqabala* (for balancing) is still reflected in the English term equal.

******

There was an important reason why this math genius developed the concepts of linear equations and their solutions. That was the complexity of the Islamic Inheritance Laws.

27

Islam, a couple of centuries old and a nascent religion then, was entering into its golden age. According to the Islamic Laws, when a Muslim died, the duties to be executed included payment of funeral expenses, payment of debts, execution of will, and the distribution of the remaining property amongst the nine Quranic heirs. Only a third of the property could be assigned by a will, and the remaining were left by Shariah Law to nine heirs, including mother, father, husband, widow, daughter, uterine brother, full sister, uterine sister, and consanguine sister. The share for the men was twice that of the women.

The complexity of these inheritance rules gave an impetus to his work on algebra. He devoted a full chapter in his book on ways to conduct inheritance calculations. However, Al Khwarizmi used descriptive terms for the elements that he worked with; not the simpler symbols like *a*, *b*, *x*, *y*, etc. that we use in algebra today.

The Spanish and Portuguese words for digit (*guarismo* and *algarismo*) still reflect the continuing influence of Al Khwarizmi. Today, a 500-kilometer double ringed basin with a 65-kilometer crater on the far side of the moon carries the name of this great mathematician.

******

Leonardo Fibonnaci (1170 AD – 1250 AD), of Pisa, Italy, later used many of Al Khwarizmi's techniques (including the Hindu-Arabic numerals) and introduced this Arab genius to the Western world.

The Arab-Indian system of numerical representation had remarkable advantages over the Greek and the Roman numbering systems.

The Greek System was primarily geometric (for example, $a + b$ was treated as adding the lengths of two lines, a and b).

The Roman System lacked zeroes and used certain placement of numbers as subtractive. For example, $X - I = IX$ (nine, with I before X) versus $X + I = XI$ (eleven, with I after X).

Both were complex systems to do anything beyond simple calculations.

******

The work on numerals and algebra by Fibonacci in the 12th century, based on Al Khwarizmi's work, inspired countless western mathematicians to look for techniques and tools to solve even larger problems.

Four centuries after Fibonacci, a Scotsman named Napier, defined a fantastic technique to simplify complex calculations.

Napier's techniques would influence calculations for the next four centuries. His pivotal story is next.

******

CHAPTER 9
MACHINE TO COUNT AND
MULTIPLY

For five millennia, abacuses of some form or shape had aided the human need to count.

The abacus may have started as lines drawn in the sand, with stones placed on the lines to represent numbers. Eventually these techniques transformed into wooden counting frames that could be carried around.

Though the abacus aided in counting, adding and subtracting, it was not useful for multiplication or division.

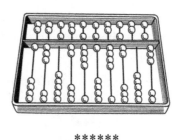

******

Then, in the 16th century, John Napier of Scotland proposed the concept of logarithms (from *logos and arithmos,* meaning proportion and number) to reduce multiplication and division to easier operations of addition and subtraction.

******

Napier's logarithm technique was almost immediately mechanized by a device called the slide rule, which continued to be in use until the 20th century. However, the logarithm tables were more accurate than slide rules.

The logarithm and trigonometric tables became fundamental to everyone – for sailors to navigate, for military to aim artillery, for bankers to calculate interest and for engineers to build.

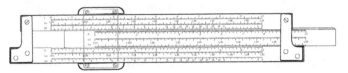

However, logarithm tables had finite accuracy (in terms of the number of decimal places that were allowed), and contained numerous errors.

Though approximate calculations were enough for most purposes, as time went by, the accuracy provided by logarithm tables became insufficient for many tasks.

******

Napier had also devised a calculation device that consisted of a board with many rods (called Napier Bones) based on the Indian lattice multiplication technique of *Bhaskara*. This device could calculate products and quotients of numbers, as well as square roots (though it did not use Napier's logarithms).

******

Within years of Napier's proposal of logarithms, Schickard combined the idea of Napier Bones and automated it further to create the Calculating Clock, which could add and subtract six-digit numbers. The system could handle carrying numbers to the next position, just like the mechanical odometers in the cars of today.

Schickard even proposed to Johannes Kepler to use this machine to create astronomical tables. Kepler, the famous astronomer who discovered the laws of planetary motion, had been involved in creating the Rudolphine Tables, named after Emperor Rudolf II, which detailed positions of planets and thousands of stars.

******

After two decades of Schickard's work, Blaise Pascal came out with the *Pascaline*, which was a calculating device that he hoped would assist his father, a tax commissioner. Though not a commercial success (since it could only add or subtract), it was notable for its use of the carry system.

But Pascaline influenced another pivotal personality and a great mind: Gottfried Leibniz.

******

> *"... It is beneath the dignity of excellent men to waste their time in calculation when any peasant could do the work just as accurately with the aid of a machine."*
>
> – *Gottfried Leibniz*

Gottfried Leibniz (1646 – 1716), who popularized the elongated S for the integration sign (from the Latin *summa*, for sum), was probably the most significant figure to influence modern computing.

Leibniz wanted an easy, fast, and reliable calculating machine. He invented and perfected over a period of twenty years, a machine called the Stepped Reckoner

33

(or Stepped Drum) – the first calculator that could conduct addition, subtraction, multiplication and division.

A pedometer that Leibniz had seen in Paris, and his readings about Pascaline, had influenced his design of the Stepped Reckoner. His approach was to add multiplying and dividing mechanisms to the basic design of the Pascaline.

However, the device lacked a key component – the carry mechanism.

******

Leibniz was a pivotal personality in the history of computing not for his calculating machine, but for the documentation of the binary system for the first time.

He conjured up designs of computing devices that used marbles, driven by gravity through pipes and holes, which could perform some of the algebraic operations.

His visions were strangely close to the computers of today, which are driven by electrons that move among holes in transistor devices and other electronics.

Leibniz also touched upon the concept of *feedback*, yet another important aspect of today's computer-based control systems.

******

The brilliant devices that Schickard, Pascal, and Leibniz created lacked a critical ability: the ability to program logic.

It would take over two more centuries for the concept of machines with programmable logic to become *even a dream*.

******

Though machines were being made to aid calculations before the 18th century, even the basic symbolic notations were only evolving. Many of the standard mathematical notations that we use today were formed over the 18th and 19th centuries, developed primarily by Euler (like *x, y, z, e, a, b, c, sigma (Σ), i, π* and *f(x)*) and some others.

The development of varied flavors of numbering systems, algebra, and standard notations solved a myriad of problems. But they were very unwieldy to be automated: because of two reasons.

The first reason was the universal dependence on analog logic in machines, which made them complex and inaccurate.

The second reason was the large number of states and combinations required to represent most numbering systems.

The solutions to these needed to wait for centuries, for a digital world and a digital thinking, based on a simple binary system with two states: ON and OFF.

Until then, the world immersed itself into symbolic thinking with formulae and rules of thumb – which were much more suited for human thought than 'thinking' machines.

******

CHAPTER 10
THE BIRTH OF MODERN COMPUTING

So how did cloth-making influence automation of computing?

In the 19th century, Joseph Marie Jacquard invented the *Jacquard Loom* to simplify the process of manufacturing textiles with intricate patterns.

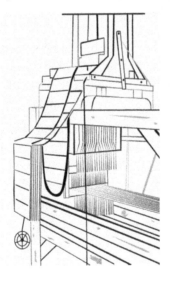

A series of replaceable pasteboard cards with punched holes (called *punched cards*) controlled the loom. The design made by the loom could be changed by changing the punched cards.

******

Charles Babbage joined Cambridge a few years after Jacquard's loom was introduced in France.

The fact that you could change the patterns woven by the loom simply by changing the punched cards, was an interesting insight for Babbage.

He theorized that if machines could be fed new logic using punched cards; then such a machine could effectively be *reprogrammed* to do different things as desired.

******

The first machine that Babbage focused on was the *Differential Engine*, for one simple reason: calculations in those days were done primarily using logarithmic and trigonometric tables.

These tables have been the central aspect of routine computation ever since Napier had brought them into the limelight. Babbage was concerned about the dangers posed by incorrect tables, which were being used at that time in almost all aspects of Western life.

To mitigate the risks, he started to devise a machine that could generate accurate tables.

He started off by eliminating the need for multiplication and division in his machine to generate such tables, by using a technique called *finite differences*. This he thought would keep the design simple.

> *"I wish to God these calculations had been executed by steam."*
>
> *- Charles Babbage*

Think about a time before electric lights, in a world still powered by steam engines.

Babbage was working with tools that were powered by steam. His designs were driven by many complex sets of gears; yet had elements of data memory, program memory, control units, conditional loops and I/O units.

BABBAGE'S ANALYTICAL ENGINE	CONTEMPERORY COMPUTER.
ACCIDENTAL SIGN	SIGN BIT
ANALYST	PROGRAMMER
ATTENDANT	OPERATOR
AXIS	BUFFER REGISTER
BARREL	MICROCODE
CARD	INSTRUCTION
CARD, OPERATION	ARITHMETIC INSTRUCTION
CARD, COMBINATORIAL	INSTRUCTION CONTROL TRANSFER (TEST / JUMP)
CARD, NUMBER	INSTRUCTION, LOAD IMMEDIATE
CARD, VARIABLE	INSTRUCTION, LOAD/STORE
CARRIAGE	CARRY PROPAGATION
CURVE DRAWING APPARUTUS	PLOTTER
COLUMN (OF RACK)	MEMORY (RAM) CELL
CYCLE	LOOP
MILL	ARITHMETIC AND LOGICAL UNIT (ALU)
RACK (OF COLUMNS)	RANDOM ACCESS MEMORY (RAM)
RUN UP	OVERFLOW OR SIGN BIT CONDITION CODE
STEPPING DOWN	RIGHT SHIFT
STEPPING UP	LEFT SHIFT
STORE	MEMORY (RAM) ARRAY
TURN OF THE HANDLE	CLOCK CYCLE

******

Yet a reconstruction of Babbage's steam-age Difference Engine, made by the London Science Museum in 1991 using 19th century construction techniques, gave results accurate up to 31 decimal places – which is far better than modern-day calculators.

******

Babbage soon shifted his attention to the more interesting Analytical Engine. This contraption was a more complex machine that could change its logic based on punched cards, as did the Jacquard Loom. In fact, the Analytical Engine may have been the first conceptual, programmable computer.

Babbage's design could conduct branching, looping, and sequential control, but was still analog in nature. Babbage even envisioned sets of punched cards as function-libraries, much like software libraries of today.

The Analytical Engine that Babbage dreamed up was never built. Yet Babbage had by now defined a *concept* that would slowly evolve into a machine called a *computer*.

******

We know of Babbage's machines today because of one woman – a countess with an eye for counting and logic. Let us meet her next.

******

CHAPTER 11
THE COUNTESS OF LOVELACE

Lord Byron, the gifted 18th century British poet, had a rather unhappy and stormy marriage with Annabella. Within a year of their marriage, Annabella decided to leave him, taking their newborn child with her. Lord Byron had wanted a son and was mired in deep financial difficulties. His behavior had turned volatile, and Annabella suspected that he was turning mad.

Annabella was adamant about her daughter, August Ada, not following her father's footsteps. She did not want Lord Byron's behavioral problems to come back and haunt her daughter's life.

Annabella ensured that Ada was given training mostly in mathematics and sciences, rather than arts and literature. That way, Annabella thought, Ada may not end up as a volatile literary figure like Lord Byron.

Yet, today Ada is best known for her *writings*.

******

Ada's legacy continues in her notes and articles detailing Charles Babbage's work. Let us delve into some of her work.

Ada noted the following in the *Sketches of the Analytical Engine*, when comparing Differential and Analytical Engines: "The Analytical Engine is not merely adapted for tabulating the results of one particular function, but for developing and tabulating *any function* whatever. In fact the engine may be described as being the material expression of *any indefinite function of any degree of generality and complexity*."

She observed that the Analytical Engine proposed by Babbage was tending to the idea of a "*thinking* or *reasoning*" machine.

******

Any machine can be seen as an expression of an algorithm to achieve a specific function. But changing the *logic* in a machine *that it was not custom-built for*, was the most notable aspect about the Analytical Engine.

******

Ada described Babbage's machine as a "mill" that operated on variables, which was fed (powered?) via supplying-cards ("food"). She said that the "mill" stored the temporary and final results in receiving-cards. The terms used by Ada reflects and contrast a time in the past, when such concepts as a computer did not even make sense!

******

Ada noted that the Analytical Engine wove *algebraic patterns*, just as the Jacquard Loom wove flowers and leaves.

A woven portrait of Jacquard himself made with a Jacquard Loom, she observed, required 24,000 cards. This, she suggested with deep insight, could be avoided with the concept of looping (*cycles*) or branching (*backing*), as was the case with the Analytical Engine.

She envisioned three cards replacing a thousand or a million cards with the use of looping and branching in the analytical engine.

******

In her final notes on Analytical Engine, she wrote an algorithm to calculate Bernoulli's Equations, which is considered to be the very first computer program every written by any human.

Number of Operation	Nature of Operation	Variables acted upon	Variables receiving results	Indication of change in the value on any variable	Statement of Results	Data ${}^1V_1$ $\bigcirc$ 0 0 1 $\boxed{1}$	${}^1V_2$ $\bigcirc$ 0 0 2 $\boxed{2}$	^{1} $\bigcirc$ (
1	$\times$	${}^1V_2 \times {}^1V_3$	${}^1V_3, {}^1V_4, {}^1V_6,$	$\left\{ \begin{array}{l} {}^1V_2 = {}^1V_2 \\ {}^1V_3 = {}^1V_3 \end{array} \right\}$	$= 2n$	. . . . .	2	
2	−	${}^1V_4 - {}^1V_1$	${}^2V_4$	$\left\{ \begin{array}{l} {}^1V_4 = {}^2V_4 \\ {}^1V_1 = {}^1V_1 \end{array} \right\}$	$= 2n-1$	1	. . . . .	. .
3	+	${}^1V_5 - {}^1V_1$	${}^2V_5$	$\left\{ \begin{array}{l} {}^1V_5 = {}^2V_5 \\ {}^1V_1 = {}^1V_1 \end{array} \right\}$	$= 2n+1$	1	. . . . .	. .
4	÷	${}^2V_5 \div {}^2V_4$	${}^1V_{11}$	$\left\{ \begin{array}{l} {}^2V_5 = {}^0V_5 \\ {}^2V_4 = {}^0V_4 \end{array} \right\}$	$= \frac{2n-1}{2n+1}$	. . . . .	. . . . .	. .
5	+	${}^1V_{11} + {}^1V_2$	${}^2V_{11}$	$\left\{ \begin{array}{l} {}^1V_{11} = {}^2V_{11} \\ {}^1V_2 = {}^1V_2 \end{array} \right\}$	$= \frac{1}{2} \cdot \frac{2n-1}{2n+1}$	. . . . .	2	. .

First Computer Program by Countess Lovelace to calculate Bernoulli Number.

She also noted in a very practical manner, that it is desirable to guard against the temptation to exaggerate the powers of the engine. She continued, "In considering any new subject, there is frequently a tendency, first, to *overrate* what we find to be already interesting or remarkable; and, secondly, by a sort of natural reaction, to *undervalue* the true state of the case…"

Her foresight on things to come was obvious in her statement: "We might even invent laws for series or formulae, and set the engine to work upon them, and thus deduce numerical results which we might not otherwise have thought of obtaining…"

Ada, the very first programmer ever, lived in a time when a thinking machine was unthinkable. Her laser-like vision and insights laid the foundation of modern day computing.

The ADA language – used primarily by the military establishment – is named after this genius. Her face now adorns most certificates of authenticity Microsoft issues for its software.

******

In spite of Annabella's best efforts, Ada exhibited many of Lord Byron's inclinations and amassed huge debts towards the end of her life. Ada died of uterine cancer at 36, the same age at which her father also had passed away.

******

The Jacquard Loom and the writings of the Countess of Lovelace, would eventually work its way into a machine that would count the population of an entire country. That's next.

******

CHAPTER 12
HOW TO COUNT EVERYONE

The United States Constitution mandates that the population of the country be counted every 10 years. The census results forms the basis for allotting congressional seats, electoral votes, government funding, etc.

The first census of 1790 counted the population of the United States at around four million. By 1880, the tenth census had counted about 50 million.

It took almost seven years to tabulate the results of the tenth census. This raised concerns that the census of 1890 would overrun the next ten years.

******

The punched cards in Jacquard's Loom had heavily influenced Charles Babbage's design of his Analytical Engine. Herman Hollerith, who worked at the Census Bureau, was inspired by the same punched cards while creating a tabulating and sorting machine to solve the enormous census problem.

With the automation devised by Hollerith, the 1890 census was tabulated within a year. This remarkable achievement added *data management* as a significant aspect of computing; along with the ability to generate tables that Babbage had devised.

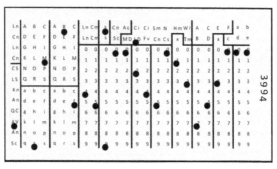

******

Hollerith's name can still be seen in modern day FORTRAN language formatting commands as in:

```
1005 FORMAT(1H ,3I3,/1H ,4F7.3)
```

1H in the above FORTRAN format syntax means a space, where H is called a Hollerith.

******

Tabulating Machine Company, the company that Hollerith formed, would eventually morph into a giant named International Business Machines Corporation, or IBM.

And as IBM was morphing into a giant, some people started paying more attention to a long-forgotten numbering system: the binary system.

******

CHAPTER 13
BINARY SYSTEMS

Most natural processes are continuous. That may have caused people to design most machines as analog devices, which are naturally continuous.

Automation of processes was invariably dependent on simple analog mechanisms like pulleys and gears.

Even the earliest attempts at computing followed this analog thinking. However, such devices quickly became very complex, even to achieve small tasks.

It would take several paradigm shifts before analog thinking turned digital, and binary numbers became the *lingua franca* of machines.

******

Cultures around the world never took binary system seriously; they did not find it convenient or useful for practical purposes.

About 2500 years ago in Ancient India, Pingala did some work on Vedic verses using short and long syllables. That may have been the first conceptual use of binary systems in human history.

In the 17th century, Francis Bacon, from England, devised a system to represent *letters* as a sequence of binary digits. For examples, 'a' may be '00000' and 'b' maybe '00001'. This technique was later reflected in standards like ASCII (American Standard Code for Information Interchange) to represent characters. Morse Code also used a variant of the binary system to represent letters.

Another 17th century genius Leibniz, from Germany, proposed the binary system with 0 and 1, to represent *numbers*.

British mathematician George Boole followed with an algebraic system of binary *logic* (called Boolean Algebra) in the 1850s. This form of logic acted on variables that took the values *true* or *false*, and were driven by operations such as *NOT*, *OR*, *XOR*, and *AND*.

Boolean algebra and binary system would later become the fundamental pieces in the design of 20th century electronics and computing marvels. However, it was a young man from Michigan who brought together boolean algebra, binary systems and electric circuits into a fascinating combination.

******

Claude Shannon was introduced to Boolean algebra in a philosophy class at the University of Michigan, in 1934.

During his master's work at MIT in 1937, Shannon was attempting to simplify the layout of electromechanical telecommunication switches and circuitry, using binary arithmetic and Boolean algebra when he suddenly realized something extraordinary. He realized that by reversing the technique, *he could solve Boolean algebra problems using electromechanical switches and circuits*. This was indeed an extraordinary insight.

Shannon's landmark work, detailed in his master's thesis launched the modern era of digital circuit design. Many still consider it the most significant master's thesis of the last century.

******

Over a period of four centuries, humanity had developed a new numbering and logic system that electric machines could begin to understand.

The transition of *numbers*, *letters* and *logic* into sets of 0s and 1s, is the basis of today's computing machinery. In fact, in today's world everything including music, movies, books and pictures, is digitized into binary code.

But it would take a very frustrated scientist in Iowa to make the world think seriously about bits, nibbles, and bytes in the design of thinking machines.

******

CHAPTER 14
ABC

John Atanasoff was fascinated (and frustrated at the same time) with the Monroe Calculator he was using for his work at the Iowa State University. He wanted something much better, but was not quite sure what.

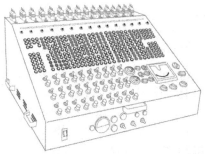

He had developed an analog geometric surface calculator called the *laplaciometer* (to solve Laplace Equations). The accuracy of analog computers was highly dependent on the quality of parts used to manufacture the device. Atanasoff felt that this was a major issue.

After a stressful day in 1937, he took his car and drove 200 miles with no intended destination, just to concentrate on something other than his work. He ended up at a brightly lit roadhouse in the State of Illinois. It was already very dark.

After a couple of drinks of bourbon, he felt relaxed. He started thinking deeper and deeper into how things could be done differently. That night, Atanasoff came out with several brain waves that would completely change computer design.

******

The most significant breakthrough he made was the proposal to use binary system to represent all the data in a computer. This was a massive shift away from the workings of previous analog computer models, which represented numbers based on the angle of rotation of a drum, or some such analog physical setting.

The second significant breakthrough was the use of electronic switches that controlled the flow of electricity (instead of mechanical elements like gears) to control and calculate. Atanasoff envisaged the use of valves rather than electro mechanical relays to enhance the speed of computation.

The third was to use a capacitor with a power boosting mechanism to function as a memory drum. Though he had decided to use 0 (absence of charge) and 1 (presence of charge) stored in capacitors to represent digits, he knew that capacitors tended to lose their stored charge (representing 1). He solved the problem by a technique called *jogging*, which refreshed the charges occasionally so that the capacitors held their state.

These were absolutely stunning changes in the race to automate the brain. The fantastic breakthroughs Atanasoff made in 1937, still drive designs and architectures of the thinking machine.

The human race had finally switched to the digital age. The rumbles of the Second World War had begun in Europe, and the race to thinking machines as we know today, was on.

******

CHAPTER 15
THE RACE FOR THE
MECHANICAL BRAIN

At the 1936 Berlin Olympics, Jesse Owens lit the race tracks on fire.

Hitler was well on his way to absolute power in Germany, amassing a huge army that would later threaten the whole world.

Amid the war clouds, three threads of thought took flight towards a single idea.

Each wanted a faster and sharper way to compute.

******

The next ten years would see the worst war the world had ever seen, and the most brilliant machines ever made.

The war engulfed the whole world – a war waged from brains that went mad.

But another war was launched by some constructive minds – a race to make the most creative machines ever assembled by man. Scientists in Germany,

England and United States worked hard toward the same fantasy – a better way to compute.

******

In 1936, Alan Turing first described a *theoretical machine* that could do it all. He called it the Turing Machine, and it could run any well-formed series of instructions – in theory.

John von Neumann expanded the *concept* to define a new architecture for future machines that could think – a memory that stored data and instructions, a processor, a logic unit, and input and output.

Though theoretical concepts when formulated, the Turing Machine and von Neumann Architectures were significant in differentiating *fixed program devices* from *freely programmable devices* that we now call computers.

Until then, computers were *mono-function* devices: like calculators, planimeters, etc. A freely programmable device meant that computers could become anything a user or designer wanted it to be – an *Omni-Functional* device.

******

In 1936, Konrad Zuse, a brilliant painter, sculptor, and civil engineer from Germany, built an electro-mechanical computer in his parent's attic. He called it the Z1.

Soon the war would cut him off from the rest of the world, but by 1942, he had made the better Z3, though it was still not entirely electronic.

******

After his brainwaves at the roadhouse in Illinois in 1937, John Atanasoff succeeded in building an electronic binary-computing machine by 1941, called ABC (Atanasoff Berry Computer). This machine was not programmable, but was possibly the first binary computer.

******

In the United States, Howard Aiken built the Harvard Mark I, along with Grace Hopper in 1944.

One day in 1945, Grace noticed that an insect had brought down her machine, thus coining the popular term "bug" in a program.

It was Grace who first suggested that machine-coding be done in clear English-like language rather than cryptic assembly languages. With this insight, she developed the world's first compiler – a program to convert programs written in human understandable language to machine readable binary code.

******

Eckert and Mauchly made ENIAC, a general-purpose computer in 1946. Mauchly was heavily influenced by Atanasoff's ideas, which he used to create the decimal-based ENIAC, and later, the binary EDVAC.

******

During the course of the war, machines were becoming binary beasts – keen on shaping a world driven by them.

The war clouded the developmental efforts, but the desire to break the encrypted codes of the enemy may have resulted in Colossus Mark I and Mark II (both in 1944) in the UK.

By 1951, variants of the Mark computer (which was developed at the Manchester University) were available from Ferranti. The Ferranti Mark I was the world's first commercially available computer.

******

By 1953, two scientists in England, Watson and Crick, published their model of the DNA Double Helix structure, in the journal *Nature*.

As the code of life etched in carbon was being decoded by molecular biologists, another bunch of geniuses were engaged in a race to transfer everything they knew into silicon.

Life was about to be changed forever by the newly created binary beasts, just as life itself was beginning to be deciphered in the labs.

******

Two of the engineers who designed the Ferranti Mark computers, Conway Berners-Lee and Mary Lee Woods, had a baby in 1955. They named him Tim, whom we will meet decades later.

******

While these huge, building-size computers were being built, many geniuses – like Vannevar Bush – had already started thinking about machines that would not only compute, but also think and interact.

******

CHAPTER 16
AS WE MAY THINK

James Thomson, Lord Kelvin's brother, had invented a mechanical analog computer called the Differential Analyzer back in 1876. The device could solve differential equations using integration.

Vannevar Bush (who later founded the National Science Foundation in the United States) had taken interest in Thompson's work. In 1927, Bush started working on improving Thompson's device.

******

Claude Shannon, who joined Bush's team to work on the Differential Analyzer, observed a beautiful way to simplify the circuitry of Bush's device using Boolean Logic. This resulted in Shannon's landmark thesis work that completely turned around designs of thinking machines ever since.

******

In 1945, Bush wrote an article proposing a device, "In which an individual stores all his books, records, and communications, and which is mechanized so that it may be consulted with exceeding speed and flexibility." The article was titled *As We May Think*. Bush had originally written the article in 1936, but decided to publish it only after a decade.

Augmented memory or *memex* as Bush called it, was based on microfilms. He envisioned: "Wholly new forms of Encyclopedia will appear, ready made with a mesh of associative trails running through them, ready to be dropped into the memex and there amplified."

His imagination ran wild. "A library of a million volumes could be compressed into one end of a desk," he wrote. He foresaw a machine that would think just as we may think!

His article appeared in July 1945. Hitler had just recently killed himself, and the next month World War II would end with Japan's surrender.

61

Bush meant his article to exhort a war-tired-generation to a knowledge revolution. But what Bush had just defined, with his laser-sharp vision, was a *hypertext system*.

******

Bush's vision inspired many, like the visionary genius we'll meet next.

******

CHAPTER 17
PEN FILLED WITH LIGHT

Doug Engelbart was a radar technician in the US Navy. His ship was enroute to the Philippines when the Captain announced, "Japan just surrendered!"

There was firecrackers and screams all over the deck.

Later, at a transit base located on a small island, Doug made his way to a tiny hut on stilts on a small island. It was the local Red Cross Library. There he picked up a magazine called *Life*.

He came across a fascinating article inside that magazine that implanted a firm vision in his mind. The article was about Vannevar Bush's *As We May Think*.

That article would change Doug's life forever.

He devoted the next years of his life to simplifying human-machine interfaces and communication.

By 1960, with a PhD in his hand and a vision in his mind, he cooked up devices and ideas that would change the way the world interacted with machines.

With his radar-technician background, he knew more about display devices than most others. He had seen the use of light pens in radar systems. With that knowledge, he imagined friendly human-computer interfaces where users thought in two dimensions, or even three.

The ideas he developed included a bit-mapped screen, multiple windows interacting with each other, crude hypertext, groupware, and a graphical user interface (GUI).

And then he also developed the invention that he is most well-known for.

A device that moved a cursor on Doug's graphical user interface screen, consisting of a wooden box with a wheel and a long tail.

A computer mouse! Just like a light pen in the radar world.

******

The story of Doug Engelbart does not stop there. He would appear again a decade later in the story of the *Intergalactic Computer Network*.

******

"We choose to go to the moon. We choose to go to the moon in this decade and do the other things, not because they are easy, but because they are hard, because that goal will serve to organize and measure the best of our energies and skills, because that challenge is one that we are willing to accept, one we are unwilling to postpone, and one which we intend to win, and the others, too."

-   *John F. Kennedy,*
    Houston, Texas,
    12 September 1962

CHAPTER 18
INTERGALACTIC COMPUTER
NETWORK

"To The Members and Affiliates of the Intergalactic Computer Network," began the memo from JCR Licklider to the rest of the Advanced Research Projects Agency (ARPA) team in 1963.

Lick, as his friends called him, was the son of an insurance salesman.

And Lick knew how to sell his ideas to an audience who was far behind the times.

******

After the Korean War in the early 50s, the United States Air Force developed SAGE (Semi-Automatic Ground Environment) – a computer-aided radar network system to warn about impending aerial attacks.

The SAGE network spanned 24 high-computing centers, and was connected by telephone lines and powered by 275-ton mammoth AN/FSQ-7 computers, which consumed 3MW of power each. It was a real-time, interactive response system against a cold unpredictable enemy.

******

Lick was involved in the SAGE project. SAGE triggered his interest in computers. He decided to acquire a PDP-1 (*Programmed Data Processor*-1 from Digital) for twenty-five thousand dollars when he joined *Bolt, Beranek and Newman* (also known as BBN, based in Cambridge, Massachusetts, USA) in 1957.

******

BBN had started off as an acoustical consulting company, and had underwent a transformation into a general high tech company.

Lick had a PhD in psychoacoustics, a good reason why BBN looked interesting to him.

Acoustic calculations required heavy computation – a good reason why Lick could easily persuade BBN to be the very first customer for a PDP-1.

Lick loved to show off the PDP-1 machine. He was the very first to publicly demonstrate time-sharing in the early 60s using this machine.

******

In 1963, Lick was appointed the head of the Behavioral Sciences and Command and Control programs at ARPA.

Today's DARPA (Defense Advanced Research Projects Agency), was then called ARPA. ARPA was the agency responsible for the development of new technologies for the military.

******

Lick was more of a visionary. He believed in man-computer symbiosis, rather than the replacement of man with machines. His visions of online communities, ways of human-interaction in a connected world, and computer interfaces may have looked outrageous in those days; but they look just ordinary in today's world.

In 1965, Lick even described the concept of "an active desk with a display-and-control system in a telecommunication-telecomputation system with a connection to a precognitive utility net that will connect to everyday business, industrial, government, and professional information, and perhaps, also to news, entertainment, and education."

That looks very much like today's Internet. But he was envisioning it in 1965.

Then Lick predicted something totally outlandish. He wrote, "A very important part of each man's interaction with his on-line community will be mediated by his OLIVER. An OLIVER is, or will be when there is one, an '*On-Line Interactive Vicarious Expediter and Responder*,' a complex of computer programs and data that resides within the network and acts on behalf of its principal, taking care of many

69

minor matters that do not require his personal attention and buffering him from the demanding world. 'You are describing a secretary,' you will say. But no! Secretaries will have OLIVERS."

ONE MESSAGE PROCESSOR
CAN BE THE MESSENGER BETWEEN
TWO OTHER MESSAGE PROCESSORS

Well, we're not yet at the age of OLIVER, though Lick foresaw it in 1965. But we surely will be there someday!

******

Lick's leadership was critical to the formulation of a communication network later called ARPANET.

The visions of Lick and Bob Taylor eventually culminated in a network design that consisted of small computers called IMPs (Interface Message Processors).

An IMP was similar to today's network routers. Making the IMPs into a different computer device (compared to having it as an integral part of the machine) was a paradigm shift in itself.

After a bidding process that included 140 potential bidders, BBN was finally given the contract from ARPA to create the IMP devices for ARPANET.

BBN chose a version of Honeywell DDP-516 computer to create the first generation IMP design. Only four such IMPs were deployed.

The first IMP was deployed at Leonard Kleinrock's lab at University of California in Los Angeles (UCLA).

The second IMP was deployed at Doug Engelbrat's (yes, the radar engineer who made the wooden box with a tail) lab at the Stanford Research Institute (SRI).

The third IMP went to University of California at Santa Barbara (UCSB).

And the fourth IMP went to University of Utah.

The Internet was finally forming, one node at a time.

******

Until then, network connectivity (like in telecommunication networks) had been setup using *circuit switching*, where a dedicated connection was established between nodes until the conversation was over.

Packet switching was a new concept that required a different kind of thinking. Communication between nodes shared the network hardware and routers to transmit packets of information that were disassembled at source, transmitted and routed through the network, received in pieces at the destination, and then reassembled back into one piece. The main advantage of this technique was that the network could be shared. But the disadvantage was that the packets would get lost or delayed, affecting the transfer rate.

From the old standard of circuit switching telecommunication systems, the world was slowly entering the age of packet switching networks. But for a moment the world was gripped by a fever – man was landing on the moon.

******

"Houston, Tranquility Base here. The Eagle has landed…

…

…

That's one small step for man, one giant leap for mankind."

> *- Neil Armstrong,*
> *Sea of Tranquility, The Moon,*
> *21 July 1969, 0256 GMT*

CHAPTER 19
WALKING ON THE MOON

Neil Armstrong became the first human to walk on the moon on 20 July 1969. His moon-vehicle was equipped with a state-of-the-art computer, which had just 36K of memory and 2MHz of processing power!

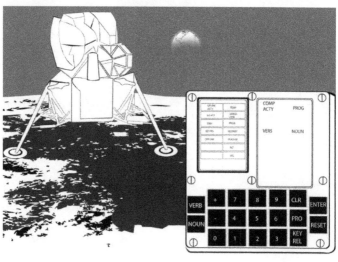

******

In just a few months, the world was also getting ready for the very first message transmission over the Internet.

On 29 October 1969, at 10:30 pm, a message was sent over the first packet switching computer network set up between Leonard Kleinrock's lab (at UCLA) and Doug Engelbart's lab (at the Stanford Research Institute). The first word sent between the two computers was '*login*'; however, after the letters *l* and *o*, the systems crashed. Hence the actual first communication between two computers over the Internet was '*lo*'.

Though the first message was a failure, Lick's vision of a communication network had materialized with those two letters. Leonard Kleinrock would be called the Father of the Internet, for the two letters he had sent.

******

BBN was the birthplace of so many ideas and inventions. In a few years, BBN would invent yet another new technology that would change the way we communicate all over again!

Life would never be the same!

******

CHAPTER 20
SNAILS AND SPAM

Ray Tomlinson and Jeff Burchfiel were colleagues at BBN.

"Do not tell anyone; this is not what we are supposed to be working on," Ray told Jeff, after showing him a program that he had developed combining a file transfer program (CPYNET) (that worked between computers) and a message sending program (SNDMSG) (that worked within a computer).

Until that day, many systems, like the Compatible Time Sharing System (CTSS) at MIT, allowed users to communicate within the same machine, but not between different computers.

That day in late 1971, Ray was able to send an *email* to another machine, just by combining two unrelated programs.

******

Ray had used the notation user@machine to indicate the receiving party, similar to the CPYNET notation. That format would later change.

There had been several moves to get rid of the '@' sign from keyboards in the 70s, and the accidental use of the sign in the email notation by Ray possibly saved it from extinction.

The very first message sent between the two computers was some uppercase gibberish (some say that it was 'QWERTYUIOP'). We can safely say that the birth of email, started with spam, :-).

******

CHAPTER 21
EMOTIONAL BLACKMAIL

```
----------------------------
19-Sep-82 11:44    Scott E   Fahlman
:-)
From: Scott E Fahlman <Fahlman at
Cmu-20c>

I propose that the following
character sequence for joke markers:

:-)

Read it sideways.
Actually, it is probably more
economical to mark things that are
NOT jokes, given current trends.
For this, use

:-(
----------------------------
```

Yes, Scott Fahlman, a Computer Scientist at CMU, gave computers that emotional connection, a smiley, in 1982, almost a decade after the first email was sent.

******

The race for transferring human intelligence to machines preceded the desire to communicate over machines – as we'll see next.

******

CHAPTER 22
THE SILICON ALCHEMY

For thousands of years, man was after a magic potion that would convert anything to gold, cure any disease and provide immortality. Alchemy, though an occult practice based on poor science and impossible objectives, resulted in a branch of science that we call 'chemistry' today.

Today's inorganic chemistry owes much of its achievements to the toils of alchemists over the centuries.

Even Sir Isaac Newton searched for the philosopher's stone. No one was immune to faith in the occult.

******

The development of computer software and hardware went through a similar phase: the search for replacing human intelligence with machine-based artificial intelligence.

The Silicon Alchemy lasted for decades.

John McCarthy coined the term artificial intelligence in 1956, as "The science and engineering of making intelligent machines."

For decades, the computer world sought expert systems, natural language processing, speech recognition, machine learning, reasoning & planning, motion & manipulation, robotics, etc. With techniques ranging from neural networks to fuzzy logic and with languages ranging from LISP to PROLOG, the Silicon Alchemy phase of hardware and software evolution was fraught with limited results and in fact, several negative results.

******

Algorithmic theory solidified further with theoretical results, which concluded that it was unlikely that some problems (classified as *NP-Complete* problems) would ever be solved in reasonable polynomial times. That meant any algorithm to solve such NP-Complete problems would easily become intractable even for a small input.

For example, the apparently simple Traveling Salesman problem, "Given a list of cities and their pair wise distances, find the shortest possible tour that visits each city exactly once," was classified as NP-Complete, which meant that it was difficult to come up with a practical algorithm to solve it consistently.

Many seemingly simple problems were later classified as NP-Complete, suggesting that they were hard to solve.

Theoretical results later indicated that *if any* NP-Complete problem is ever solved in a consistent and reasonable time (as measured by a polynomial order scale for a variable input size), *then all* NP-Complete Problems could also be solved in consistent and reasonable times.

So far, no one has been able to pick up the gauntlet of solving any one of them.

******

The search for artificial intelligence never really took off.

Maybe what was missing was a truly powerful network. The push for the elixir of truly intelligent machines created more potent machines, a networked world, far better interfaces and devices, and a great medium through which to express and experience life.

Sometimes even Alchemy is good. Today's dreams of artificial intelligence would someday spawn totally unpredictable and useful innovations.

******

As machines evolved over decades, so did the way we communicated with them. That is next.

******

82

CHAPTER 23
THE BABEL

Konrad Zuse proposed the first high-level computer language in 1945, called the *Plankalkul* (Plan Calculus).

It contained concepts such as assignments, subroutines, conditional statements, loops, floating point arithmetic, arrays, data structures, exception handling and assertions – like those found in most modern programming languages.

******

John Backus proposed the Speedcoding system, followed by Formula Translation (FORTRAN) in 1953. He was also a member of the American and British team who created the ALGOL (Algorithmic Language).

John Backus was also central in defining the Backus-Naur Form (BNF), a way of expressing context-free language grammars (which simply means equations of the form $X <= Y$, where X is a single symbol, whereas Y is not and could be a long expression).

BNF meant that the left hand side of an equation in a line of code always contained a single variable, and the right hand side contained an expression of any level of complexity. This was unlike routine algebraic equations that could contain complex expressions on both sides.

By 1964, BASIC (Beginners All-purpose Symbolic Instruction Code) was developed by Kemeny and Kurtz for non-science majors. And Nicholas Wirth invented the language called Pascal in 1970.

******

In 1969, Ken Thompson and Dennis Ritchie at Bell Labs developed an Operating System called UNIX for the PDP-7 machine, based on their previous work on a Multics machine.

By 1972, they had devised the C language to aid them to move UNIX onto a PDP-11. C got its name because it was loosely based on an earlier language called B.

A decade later, Bjarne Stroustrup would add the concept of classes from a language called SIMULA, developed by Kristen Nygaard, to the C language to create C++. SIMULA had concepts like objects, classes, subclasses, virtual methods, discrete event simulation and garbage collection.

******

The new languages enabled people to think less about bits, bytes and addresses, and more about what they wanted to do.

******

A few dared to think beyond the common purposes of a calculating machine.

And there were a few people who wanted to make machines do way more than anybody dared to think. The story of one of those geniuses is next.

******

CHAPTER 24
AN APPLE A DAY

A baby boy was born on February 24, 1955 to a Syrian professor and an American graduate student. They named him Steve.

Circumstances forced the couple to put the baby up for adoption. Joanne, the biological mother, had only one condition. She wanted Steve to be adopted only by couples who were college-educated.

Steve was soon to be adopted by a lawyer and his wife. At the last moment the couple backed out, saying they wanted a girl.

******

It was midnight when Paul and Clara received a call.

"We have an unexpected baby boy; do you want him?" the caller asked.

"Yes, we would love to have him!" replied the two eagerly, with one voice.

******

The adoption process came to a halt when the biological mother realized that Paul and Clara had never finished college. After several months of negotiations the biological mother agreed to sign the adoption papers.

Under just one condition: that the child would be sent to college.

******

Paul and Clara poured all their savings into Steve's college fund. But within six months, Steve had dropped out of most of the classes he did not find interesting at the Reed College, in Portland.

He just wanted to stop spending all the money his adopted parents had saved for him, and use it wisely. He cut corners as far as he could. He stayed with his friends to save on rent. He collected coke bottles for 5c refunds. He would even walk seven miles to the local Hare Krishna Temple every Sunday for a free vegetarian meal.

With more time to spare, Steve got involved in a calligraphy class. He was fascinated by the details of typography such as serif and sans serif typefaces. He was eager to learn about what actually made some of the typefaces look so great compared to others.

******

Steve also saved enough money to make a trip to India in search of spiritual enlightenment.

When he came back in 1974, he was lucky to get a deal from Atari, a games maker, to reduce the number of silicon chips needed for its game. For every chip he could reduce, Atari offered to pay him $100.

Steve had met Woz at a summer job at Hewlett Packard (while Steve was still in high school), and he had noticed Woz's skills with electronics. Steve made a deal with Woz to split his deal with Atari 50-50.

Woz was a wiz. He reduced the number of chips by an amazing fifty, to come up with a super-compact design.

Atari paid Steve $5000. Steve paid Woz only $300.

Maybe because spreadsheets had not been invented at that time to do the calculations, :-).

******

In 1976, Steve and Woz founded Apple.

The local Byte Shop offered Steve Apple's first deal: $500 for every fully assembled computer he could supply – payment terms were 'cash on delivery' (COD).

Apple I, the first design that Steve and Woz came up with, had a TV for display and a cassette interface for loading and saving programs.

With a bank loan for $250,000 Apple was on its way to becoming a powerhouse.

******

The revolutionary ideas of Doug Engelbart had worked its way from SRI to a nearby competitor,

Xerox PARC (Palo Alto Research Center) – through some of his younger colleagues who had left the team.

The Xerox team developed a computer called Xerox Alto in 1973, inspired by Doug's mouse, GUI and desktop. Alto was the very first computer to have these awesome features.

In 1979, Xerox granted Steve and his team three-day access to its facilities for $1,000,000 of Apple pre-IPO stock – an opportunity that was used by Apple engineers to understand the details of the GUI (also called WIMP – *W*indow, *I*con, *M*enu and *P*ointing Device).

Now through Steve Jobs, Doug's revolutionary ideas were finally ready to go out to the public.

******

But Apple needed a killer app!

Dan Brickly had noticed the difficulty his Harvard Business School Professor was having in explaining the numbers on the table he had drawn on the blackboard. He had to erase, recalculate and rewrite the numbers for every change he made.

Dan started to daydream about a magical sheet of paper – a blackboard, with grids that contained a calculator and a pointing device (called mouse that he had recently seen) – all rolling into one like an "electronic paper spreadsheet."

The Visicalc spreadsheet that Dan Brickly and Bob Frankston released in 1979 for Apple Computers would push Steve's machines into something more than a toy for nerds – into a necessity for businesses worldwide.

******

Steve's interest in calligraphy finally found its way into a fascinating array of fonts in Apple computers, nicely supported by its graphical user interface.

And with Visicalc, Apple now had the killer app!

On 12 December 1980 Apple went public. Its stock opened at $14 and closed the day at $29. Valued in a day at two billion dollars, it made 300 millionaires by going public.

******

"Do you want to spend the rest of your life selling sugared water to children, or do you want a chance to change the world?" Steve Jobs asked an uncertain John Sculley.

Sculley was the president of Pepsi in 1983. Sculley took over the reins of Apple almost immediately.

Within a year and a half, John Sculley asked Steve to leave Apple. Their relationship had become coarse, and the markets were not doing too well either.

******

Steve was already onto his next idea: a company called NeXT that made interesting computers.

NeXT computer was unique for its black magnesium case, and was intended to be a truly personal computer. Its high price prevented it from becoming popular, but its user-friendly interface and communication features were noteworthy.

A few years later, Jobs' futuristic NeXT computer would become the launch pad for the most exciting development of the 20th century.

******

Jobs had purchased a third of the computer division of Lucasfilm (called the Graphics Group) for $10 million in 1986.

Later he renamed the company Pixar, and it went on to become one of the world's premier computer animated movie makers. Pixar would eventually be sold to Disney, making Jobs the largest shareholder in Disney stock.

******

Jobs would rejoin Apple in a decade, after Sculley had left the company. And Apple would once again be known as one of the most creative companies in the world: the company that gave us the iMac, the iPod and the iPhone.

******

Steve had mastered the movie world with Pixar, music world with iPod, telecommunication world with iPhone and computer world with Apple.

While Apple rose, fell and rose again, another major player was emerging in the horizon.

******

CHAPTER 25
THE BATTLE OF WILLS

"What are you doing?" demanded Mary, over the intercom.

"I am thinking," six-year-old Trey shouted back.

"You're thinking?" asked Mary.

"Yes, Mom, I am thinking. Have you ever tried thinking?" said Trey angrily.

Trey was the fourth William in the family. But his dad had dropped the title, and hence Trey was called Trey, as in "three" to indicate he was the third William in the family.

******

Mary was an outgoing personality. Trey was too quiet and reserved. His parents thought that counseling would help.

The psychologist was a fun guy. He taught Trey about Freud and psychology theory.

After many counseling sessions, the psychologist concluded that Trey was perfectly fine. He advised

Mary to accept that Trey as he was – strong-willed and intelligent just like her.

******

Seven-year-old Trey was captivated by the *World's Fair at Seattle* of 1962.

The Space Needle had just been built for the fair, but what caught Trey's fancy was the 'library of the future' shown at the American Library Association (ALA) pavilion – built around a UNIVAC computer.

A machine that could think, Trey observed.

By age nine, Trey had read the entire *World Book Encyclopedia* end-to-end.

In junior high, Trey was very small and shy and that worried his parents. So they decided to send him to an elite private school called Lakeside.

Trey was not confident in social gatherings. He would fret for days before asking a girl out to the prom, because he was afraid of being turned down.

Trey loved acting, and played the lead in a few plays at the nearby church.

But what fascinated the eighth grader the most was something in an old class room building next to the church – a teletype computer terminal that the Mother's Club had bought from the proceeds of a jumble sale.

Trey was good at the machine. He designed a tic-tac-toe program for the computer, shortly followed by a board game called Risk. The end goal of Risk was world domination.

******

Trey, Paul, Kent and Ric – now called the Lakeside Programming Group (LPG) – had gotten access to a PDP-10 computer at a company called C-Cubed. The Mother's Club fund financed their computer time. But the fund was soon exhausted, and the four resorted to manipulating the computer time logs to get more computer time. They were caught red-handed and the four were banned from using the PDP-10 that summer.

Later C-Cubed made a deal with LPG – they could use the PDP-10 for free as long as they worked on getting the system debugged, which they were very good at. Trey was clearly the leader of the pack, and soon they took over the task of making a payroll system for Information Sciences, Inc. – which gave them more computer time and money.

Others at Lakeside had started noticing the boy's skills. Trey soon got the job of writing software to schedule classes for students. He added a secret function to the scheduling software that placed him in the class with the most female students.

In the fall of 1970, LPG broke up, as Paul and Ric went off to college.

******

Kent Evans was Trey's best friend. Kent and Trey dreamed that they were going to take over the world.

Kent loved mountaineering. It helped him take his mind off of the pressures of computer programming.

Their dreams of world domination were cut short by a phone call from their headmaster.

"Kent lost his footing while climbing and fell, and he passed away in the rescue helicopter," the headmaster told Trey.

Kent's death crushed Trey. For weeks he could not even get up from his bed.

******

Trey and Paul got back together again. They started working on an Intel 8088 Microprocessor, which had recently appeared on the market. They used the device to make a traffic counting device called Traf-O-Data.

The product was a complete commercial failure.

******

With an SAT score of 1590/1600, Trey was accepted to Harvard in 1973, where he for the first time met folks who were better at math than him. And it is at Harvard that he met Steve – his future business partner.

******

In 1975, Paul saw a strange device on the cover of *Popular Electronics*. That strange blue box would change their destiny.

It was an Altair 8800, the first microcomputer available to the public. Altair was made by Micro Instrumentation and Telemetry Systems (MITS) in Albuquerque in New Mexico.

In five weeks, Paul and Trey created the first BASIC compiler for this box with flickering lights.

In 1976, Trey – also called William Henry "Bill" Gates III – flew to New Mexico, to see Paul, who had by now joined MITS.

That summer the two founded Micro-soft.

The two created a new version of BASIC, called MS-BASIC that worked for microprocessors such as Tandy, Commodore, and General Electric, as well as Altaire.

******

Bill loved fast cars, and loved to race in the deserts of New Mexico in his Porche 911. He was a risk-taker.

In 1978, Bill and Paul decided to move the headquarters to Seattle.

On the trip from Albuquerque to Seattle, Bill got three speeding tickets – two from the same cop, who had trailed him after he had gotten the first.

******

By 1980, Microsoft needed a manager to keep up with the growing business. Bill called Steve Ballmer, his Harvard classmate, to lure him to leave Proctor & Gamble and to join Microsoft.

Ballmer joined on 11 June 1980 as Microsoft's twenty fourth employee – for a salary of $50,000 per year and 8 percent of Microsoft.

In 1982, Microsoft released MS-DOS (based on QDOS, 'Quick and Dirty' Operating System) for the IBM PC. The success of the 'Personal Computer (PC)' from IBM and its clones virtually guaranteed Microsoft as a serious player in the computer industry for years to come.

In 1985, Microsoft announced Windows 1.0, a Graphical User Interface for the IBM PC, and started on a collision course with Apple, the other company with a nice graphical user interface.

******

On 13 March 1986 Microsoft went public with an IPO starting at $21 and closing at $28. Bill Gates was worth $230 million and Paul Allen was worth $130 million by the end of that day.

Microsoft would eventually make four billionaires and about 12000 millionaires over the next few decades.

In 25 years, Bill Gates would be worth about $100 billion, which is about two million dollars per hour of his career. At that rate, stopping to pick up a few hundred dollars from the floor would actually cost him more money!

In 2009, due to the downturn of the economy, his fortunes were about half of that, still close to a staggering $40 billion.

******

Around 1975, many key events took place.

Microsoft was founded.

Apple released Apple I.

And at the same time, in a remote lab in California, something else was brewing. Leonard Kleinrock, who created the world's first computer network at this lab had a student named Vint Cerf.

And Vint Cerf was cooking up what would later be called TCP/IP, the backbone of Internet protocols.

ARPANET was finally morphing into the Internet. That story is next…

******

CHAPTER 26
CERFING THE WEB

Vint Cerf, a UCLA researcher and an expert at packet switching networks, imagined a world-wide network where every machine had a 32-bit address.

That meant there could be at most 4,294,967,296 computers (2^{32}) all over the world. For all practical purposes, in 1974, this was more than enough. Cerf had thought he could provide a bigger range of addresses in a later version. Little did he expect the explosive growth of the web!

******

Each machine in the Internet has a four part address, called an IP address.

An IP Address looks like 66.66.66.66, with four numbers (each less than 256) separated by periods.

Each of the four numbers represent a network, its subnets and a host machine. Today, a combination of four such numbers direct every packet that traverses the Internet to its destination.

******

In 1982, the Network Working Groups proposed a friendlier notation to indicate machine names. ARPANET had used the notation such as *Fred@ISIF* to address a user in a machine.

This was replaced by the newer Internet notation that looked like *Fred@F.ISI.ARPA*.

There were only four top-level domain names initially: .arpa, .csnet, .bitnet, and .uucp.

In January 1985, they were replaced with: .bitnet, .com, .int, .edu, .gov, .mil, .net and .org.

And each country was also represented by its own top domain.

Now, every machine had an address like myworld.zcubes.com.

******

The very first *.edu* sites registered were cmu.edu, purdue.edu, rice.edu and ucla.edu (April 1985). The first *.gov* site was css.gov (June 1985), first *.org* site was mitre.org (July 1985) and the first *.com* site was symbolics.com (15 March 1985).

******

A major development occurred at IBM Almaden Research Center in San Jose, California, around the time Leonard Kleinrock, Doug Engelbrat and Vint Cerf had worked together, sending their first packets over the net back in 1969.

It was a strange language, called GML, created at a time when the world was focused on landing on the moon. GML would find its way into every webpage on the planet in another two decades.

******

CHAPTER 27
MARK ME UP

For centuries, in the printing and publishing world, a paper manuscript was marked up by a typographer to indicate the style, size and typeface to be applied to parts of the document. This process was often used by editors, designers, proofreaders and publishers. Every manuscript had to go through the mark up process.

Then computers appeared.

Stanley Rice, a book designer from New York, proposed the concept of universal editorial structure tags in the 1960s. It was the beginning of a trend towards separating formatting from content in documents.

******

Charles Goldfarb at IBM started working on automating law office information systems in 1969.

Along with Mosher and Lorie, Goldfarb invented GML (the name came from the first letters of their last names). GML, also called *Generalized Markup Language*, allowed text editing, formatting and retrieval in document sharing systems.

Example of GML
```
:book.
:body.
:h1.The Thinking Thing
:p. Written by Me
:ol.
:li. History of Computing
:li. Computing Now
:li. Computing Tomorrow.
:eol.
```

******

Goldfarb continued working on markup concepts such as short references, linking, document types, etc. He then invented SGML by expanding on the core GML ideas.

"In 1966, I knew nothing about computers, but I knew there had to be a better way to produce documents than dictating them, reviewing a draft, marking up the draft with corrections, reviewing the retyped draft, and then, in frustration, seeing that the typist had introduced more errors while making the corrections..."

- Charles Goldfarb,
The Roots of SGML, 1996.

SGML was accepted as a standard by the late 1970s, with entities like the IRS and the DOD adopting it as their *lingua franca* of document structure.

```
Example of SGML
<body>
<h1>The Thinking Thing</h1>
<p> Written by Me</p>
<ol>
<li>History of Computing.
<li>Computing Now.
<li>Computing Tomorrow.
</ol>
</body>
```

******

By 1986, SGML had become the accepted standard in Europe as well.

The SGML Standards Document itself was published using an SGML system that was developed by a researcher named Anders Berglund.

Anders worked for the *Conseil Européen pour la Recherche Nucleaire*, otherwise called CERN, the European Particle Physics Laboratory.

That is where Anders met Tim, a thirty-year-old from Britain, who loved a book called *Enquire Within Upon Everything*.

******

106

"Information is the oxygen of the modern age. It seeps through the walls topped by barbed wire, it wafts across the electrified borders... The Goliath of totalitarianism will be brought down by the David of the microchip."

- Ronald Reagan,
The Guardian,
London,
14 June 1989

CHAPTER 28
BIRTH OF A SPIDER WEB

```
Whether You Wish to Model a Flower in Wax;
to Study the Rules of Etiquette;
to Serve a Relish for Breakfast or Supper;
to Plan a Dinner for a Large Party or a Small One;
to Cure a Headache;
to Make a Will;
to Get Married;
to Bury a Relative;
Whatever You May Wish to Do, Make, or to Enjoy,
Provided Your Desire has Relation to the Necessities
of Domestic Life,
I Hope You will not Fail to 'Enquire Within.'
```

- From the introduction to
Enquire Within Upon Everything

The how-to book '*Enquire Within Upon Everything*' covered all aspects of domestic life, from investment, gardening, decorating, food, medicine and law, and had been popular in England since 1856. It gave information to the readers regarding anything they wanted to do.

******

Tim found the book very interesting.

It opened his mind to a magical world through this *catalogue of whatever one would want to know*.

Tim had read Arthur C. Clarke's short story "Dial F for Frankenstein" as a teenager. The story described computers that were networked together into a living breathing human brain. This idea had caught Tim's fancy.

His parents, Connie and Mary, noticed that Tim had always been fascinated by machines, especially the electronic ones.

******

In the early 1980s, Tim began working at CERN on a project to organize information. He called the system ENQUIRE, after the book he loved.

ENQUIRE, written in PASCAL language, linked documents back and forth. Each node had a title and a type. It ran on a mini-computer, *Norsk Data*, made by a Norwegian company.

******

Tim returned to CERN in 1984 after a short stint at an image processing company in England.

His interaction with Anders Berglund at CERN, may have had a profound impact on Tim.

Anders introduced Tim to the power of SGML, which by now CERN had adopted for document processing and publication.

A document written by Tim in 1986 describing a distributed system supported by multiple platforms indicates his early interest in SGML:

```
<BODY>
<H1>Introduction
This manual describes how to build a
distributed system using the Remote
Procedure Call system developed in the
Online Group of the DD Division of
CERN, the European Particle Physics
Laboratory.
<h2> The system
The remote procedure call product …
<ul>
<li>VAX/VMS,
<li>Unix (Berkley 4.3 or Ultrix or
equivalent)
<li>…
<li>The IBM-PC running Turbo-Pascal or
Turbo-C
<li>The Macintosh running Turbo-Pascal
or MPW
</ul>
etc.
```

Tim wanted to redesign the ENQUIRE system with a more distributed approach, which supported multiple operating systems.

******

He now had the three ingredients that he needed to make a revolution:

The popular *TCP/IP* by Vint Cerf to connect computers worldwide;

The flexible *SGML* by Goldfarb; and

The graphical *NeXT* machine from Steve Jobs.

One. Two. Three.

The network.

The language.

The machine.

He had it all!

> *"I just had to take the hypertext idea and connect it to the Transmission Control Protocol and domain name system ideas and — ta-da! — the World Wide Web."*
>
> *– Tim Berners-Lee*

******

By 1990, CERN had funded a six-month project to develop Tim's vision. By 1991, Tim had developed the first web server, the first web editor, the first web browser and the first web site.

On 6 August 1991, *http://nxoc01.cern.ch* went live.

******

The First Gulf War had ended just six month ago, with Saddam Hussein's defeat at the hands of the Allied Forces. The world was watching the Soviet Union collapsing in a spectacular series of events. Yet Tim's idea would eclipse everything else in the pages of history.

******

Tim had at first considered the name *The Information Mine* for the web. He turned it down since it would have abbreviated to TIM, his own name. So he chose a fascinating name: The *World Wide Web*.

The world now had a revolutionary platform that would forever change the course of human history.

******

CHAPTER 29
REVOLUTIONS NO ONE NOTICED

The silent revolution launched in 1991 by Tim Berners-Lee in a quiet city in Switzerland has changed the way we live, love and connect. It has changed the way wars are fought, won and lost.

It has forever changed the ways we trade, shop, entertain, learn, express and experience.

From then on, we have lived in a different world.

Even the disintegration and disappearance of the Soviet Union in 1991 pales in comparison to a revolution written with two simple digits, 0 and 1.

That revolution launched by Tim is now history, it is the present, and it will be the future!

******

In 1991, Tim Berners-Lee and Robert Cailliau submitted a paper describing the World Wide Web to the Hypertext '91 Conference that was to be held in San Antonio that December.

The paper was rejected because their idea was in violation of the architectural principles of the existing successful hypertext systems.

Well, go figure that one out!

******

Just 20 days after Tim's software went live, another muted announcement from Sweden would start another major revolution in software.

On 25 August 1991, Linus Torvalds announced FreaX, a free UNIX platform.

The FTP administrator, who did not like the name FreaX, put the software into a directory named Linux.

And the Linux revolution was on.

******

The net was shifting its landscape, with Tim and a few other pioneers at its helm. Let us meet a few of them next.

******

CHAPTER 30
A PICTURE IS WORTH A THOUSAND WORDS

Starting in August 1991, Tim and many others defined the new web. Over the next several years, they would discuss and decide the rules of how it would work.

New browsers came out shortly afterwards. Perry (Pei-Yuan Wei) released the first graphical browser called ViolaWWW in 1992. It was the very first web browser to support interactive embedded objects, tables, input forms, style sheets, and scripts. ViolaWWW also supported multiple fonts, visited page history, bookmarking, single click link activation, and view source functionality.

The browser, as we know it, had started crystallizing.

******

Marc Andreessen worked at the National Center for Supercomputing Applications at the University of Illinois at Urbana-Champaign, where he came to know of Tim's work. Marc Andreessen and Eric

Bina, a co-worker, started working on a user-friendly browser with integrated graphics called Mosaic.

******

Proposal of IMG tag by Marc Andreessen

Sub: proposed new tag: IMG

Marc Andreessen (*marca@ncsa.uiuc.edu*)
Thu, 25 Feb 93 21:09:02 -0800

I'd like to propose a new, optional HTML tag:
IMG
Required argument is SRC="url".
This names a bitmap or pixmap file for the browser to attempt to pull over the network and interpret as an image, to be embedded in the text
at the point of the tag's occurrence.
An example is:
<IMG SRC="file://foobar.com/foo/bar/blargh.xbm">
(There is no closing tag; this is just a standalone tag.)
This tag can be embedded in an anchor like anything else; when that happens, it becomes an icon that's sensitive to activation just like a regular text anchor.
…
Let me know what you think.........
Cheers,
Marc
--

```
Marc Andreessen
Software Development Group
National Center for Supercomputing
Applications
marca@ncsa.uiuc.edu
```

The letter above shows an exchange between Marc and the rest of the web pioneers regarding the new HTML standards. The request for the new IMG tag by Marc to show images on web pages was accepted by Tim to be added to the standards only after many objections – mostly on theoretical reasons.

******

The browser displayed text and pictures, but the need to execute programs on the server was persistent.

Marc Andreessen had rejected calls to add an exec:// command to the browser. "It's a mammoth security problem in general... the results could still be catastrophic," the security-conscious Mark wrote on 3 March 1993.

The Common Gateway Interface (CGI) was formulated towards that goal. A web request may provide parameters (through simple GET or a form POST – two techniques for a browser to talk to the server) to a program sitting on the server, and the results may be provided back to the client browser.

With CGI, the web server became more intelligent than a simple FTP file server. The CGI interface was later overrun by more efficient modules and plug-ins on the web server (like NSAPI, ISAPI, etc.).

******

In 1993, Marc graduated and left for California, where he met Jim Clarke, the founder of Silicon Graphics. Jim had been looking for something totally new. He had been frustrated, because of some internal clashes within the Silicon Graphics management.

Jim and Marc teamed up, and on 4 April 1994 they launched Mosaic Communications.

117

The company was later renamed Netscape, and went for an IPO on 9 August 1995. The stock went from $14 to $75 at close of that day, a spectacular gain. Jim Clarke had converted his $5 million investment into a cool $2 billion.

******

Meanwhile, Linux grew into a force to be reckoned with by piggy-backing on the wildly popular World Wide Web.

In 1998, Linux distributors started packaging and distributing the LAMP solution. LAMP included the *L*inux Operating System, *A*pache Web Server, *M*ySQL Database, and *P*HP/Perl/Python programming languages; the name was formed from the first letters of the four modules.

Today, Apache powers more than half of the web servers on the planet.

******

The browser was a killer application. From its birth, it started to threaten a nervous giant: Microsoft.

Sun Microsystems, a major vendor of computer hardware then, was watching. It saw an opportunity to break into the browser world, and thus into every machine.

Something really hot was brewing at Sun.

******

118

CHAPTER 31
A HOT CUP OF JAVA

James Gosling at Sun Microsystems was creating a new language that could run on a TV set-top box. He looked out of his window and saw an oak tree.

He named the language Oak. Oak ran on a virtual machine, and hence could be made to run on any machine without changing the program. Oak, though similar to C and C++ languages created by Bell Labs in the 70s, was far simpler to work with.

Gosling eventually renamed the language to Java. Java was a safe and secure way to run programs inside a webpage. Shortly after its development, every browser adopted Java as the standard to run embedded logic.

******

Microsoft now had two big threats to its survival.

One was the Netscape browser that provided a uniform interface across all operating systems.

And the second was Java, a language that was taking over the web browsers, as well as web servers.

Both Netscape and Java were out to reduce Windows, Microsoft's flagship platform, into another 'insignificant operating system'.

******

Bill Gates had refused to label the Internet browser as a 'killer-app' in his book, *The Road Ahead*, which was published on November 1995.

Instead, Bill suggested that MSN (The Microsoft Network) was the network of the future.

On 7 December 1995, within weeks of the release of his new book, seeing that Internet was clearly looming as the next big threat and opportunity, Bill Gates directed Microsoft to remake itself as an Internet-focused company.

The world had probably never witnessed such a massive and dramatic shift in strategy by any company the size of Microsoft.

The new strategy of Microsoft was to embrace-and-extend the browser, to adopt Java technology and to invest heavily in HTML enhancements to its applications.

Microsoft also decided to provide its web browser (Internet Explorer) for free, sucking the winds out of Netscape's sails.

******

The Netscape release (version 2.0B3) in December 1995 had a new feature that no one gave much attention to, though it would later change the web forever. It was a simple scripting language called Javascript, developed by Brendan Eich of Netscape.

It had initially been named Mocha, but the name was changed to Javascript to ride on the popularity of the Java language. It would take more than a decade for the true power of Javascript to come out.

******

During the browser wars, the boundaries between desktops and web-tops began to disappear.

Microsoft turned everything it had against Netscape. Pushing the envelope, both companies unleashed several years of exceptional creativity.

But Netscape's David soon lost the war against Microsoft's Goliath.

AOL acquired Netscape on 24 November 1998 in a $4.2 billion deal. And Netscape was on its way to obsolescence.

******

Looking back, there were strategies that Netscape could possibly have adopted to survive, like a search company launched from a garage would later prove. However, the unstable market, misfit within AOL and poor management decisions forced Netscape to disappear shortly thereafter.

Microsoft was now the undisputed king of the Internet.

For Microsoft, the known enemies were dead by 1998, but the victory would not last long.

******

CHAPTER 32
GOLDEN GOPHERS

Archie Andrews, the 17-year-old boy with red hair, went to Riverdale High. His best friend, Jughead, loved to eat. Archie liked Veronica Lodge, a rich brunette as well as Betty Page, a middle-class blonde.

They were cartoon characters, popular since the

1940s.

******

FTP, or File Transfer Protocol, had been the primary way to transfer and access files over the Internet prior to World Wide Web. Documents, images and programs were distributed throughout the world using public FTP directories.

The first file listing mechanism on the net was called Archie, which listed FTP directories located in machines around the world. Archie, launched in 1990, was soon followed by Gopher. Gopher was a glorified FTP listing, indexed using Veronica and Jughead search engines.

******

Gopher was very popular, and could have evolved into something like the World Wide Web. gopher:// was as ubiquitous in the academic world then, as http:// is today.

In 1993, the University of Minnesota, where Gopher was originally created to make it easier to find information on the university computers, made a fatal mistake.

It decided to charge a licensing fee.

"Greed would kill gopher," complained Paul Lindner, one of Gopher's creators.

Rob Raisch, one of the Gopher users at spdcc.com, wrote to the University in anger on 11 March 1993,

"Congratulations. You may have succeeded in accomplishing something which takes a large corporation years of practice and many hundreds of thousands of dollars to do: You've killed the product before it ever leaves your door."

John Franks of Northwestern University wrote, "I really do have a great sense of sadness about this... I had hoped that Gopher would be another success and it is disappointing to see greed wipe out that hope... Scholarly journals certainly can't afford to pay 7.5 percent of their gross receipts to the Minnesota Gopher team, not to mention the $5K annually..."

John predicted in 1993, "Maybe WWW will start to take off. Electronic publishers are very interested in SGML anyway. This is a golden opportunity for the WWW people."

******

Tim Berners-Lee had maintained a directory of web servers for months. It was soon overrun by the growth of the web itself.

The World Wide Web was initially a document storage and retrieval mechanism designed for research groups around the world.

From 1991 to 1995, the web transformed into the world's biggest research library. Most of the techniques to find information on the web were hence developed by universities around the world, than by giant computer corporations.

Beginning in 1993, several search engines were developed to index the web, including Wandex and Aliweb. Webcrawler soon became the first engine to index the text in pages.

Lycos from Carnegie Mellon, Excite from Stanford, Inktomi from UC Berkley and AltaVista from Digital blazed the trail of web search.

******

Strangely named *Yet Another Hierarchical Officious Oracle* or *Yahoo*, Jerry's guide to the World Wide Web was launched from Stanford in 1994.

In the story *Gulliver's Travels* by Jonathan Swift, Yahoos are deformed filthy humans ruled by Houyhnhnms, a race of gentle horses. The story contrasted evil-natured humans with mild-mannered horses.

And Jerry Yang and David Filo named their new company 'Yahoo!' after the evil, filthy humans.

Yahoo! classified the net, but did not do text indexing. This they left to others – a choice that later proved to be a big mistake.

******

Even Netscape did not see the significance of search. Instead, in 1996, it made a deal with Yahoo!, Magellan, Lycos, Infoseek and Excite – to feature them on a rotating basis for $5 million each per year – in its desperate (or possibly innocent) effort to somehow create business models.

Netscape was once at the center of the web. Netscape left the search business to other specialized players, to focus solely on browsing software. This decision later proved to be Netscape's big mistake.

******

And while Netscape and Yahoo! waxed and waned along with many others who were trying to be portals for everyone, a new star was rising in the search world.

******

... All the negatives add up – making the online experience not worth the trouble.

*- Wall Street Journal,
17 June 1996*

CHAPTER 33
SEARCHING FOR MAGIC

Larry Page first met Sergey Brin at Stanford in the spring of 1995. Sergey had been assigned to show Larry around the university.

Within a year, they were making a new piece of software that would index the entire Internet.

Soon their program consumed large amounts of the university's network bandwidth, as it sucked up web pages from all over the Internet. The program was soon named Google – from googol, the huge number with one followed by one-hundred zeroes.

******

Both Larry and Sergey had one goal: *to invent a searching technique that would fit a king*.

They did not care about efficiency. They wanted to create a search technique as if they had all the computing resources in the world at their disposal. Just like a king would have.

That is, everything except human intervention.

******

There were many search engines in existence by then, but Larry and Sergey knew that searching could be done in a better way.

"Not all pages are created equal," noted Sergey.

******

Their work at Stanford gave rise to an awesome idea: a way to rank pages based on their relevance.

Google's PageRank results was soon recognized as the world's best; by users worldwide who wanted relevant and quick results!

The domain *google.com* became a reality on 15 September 1997. Within a year Google, a company founded in a proverbial garage, would start to threaten the most powerful software company on Planet Earth: Microsoft.

******

Bill Gross of IdeaLabs originated the idea of pay-per-click, which spawned GoTo.com. Google's Adwords and Adsense were developed based on similar ideas, and turned out to be a resounding financial success. This gave Google its much-needed business model.

******

While some brilliant minds were helping the world to search the vast Internet, there were plans afoot to help the world buy and sell – whatever people wanted.

******

CHAPTER 34
THE RIVER OF THINGS

In 1994, Internet had been growing at 2500%.

It was a fact Jeff could not ignore.

Jeff was a computer programmer, and a businessman at heart. He had been following the revolution that had been taking place.

He considered several mail order businesses, and noticed that books had long listings of items that could not all be printed in catalogues. He thought that books could be listed on a virtual catalogue on this new medium called the World Wide Web.

The business plan was clear to Jeff. It was a winner.

He could visualize the long listings of books with small thumbnails of cover pages and comments and ratings from buyers to aid another buyer. It was a game waiting to be played out.

But Jeff did not know much about the book business.

So he headed to a convention of American Booksellers in Los Angeles. There he learned that most book sellers already had electronic catalogues.

The next step, he figured out, was to bring all of them together into one place, and open the shop for business.

Jeff and his wife decided that this is exactly what they would do.

They took a Chevy and headed to Seattle, the city where Ingram Publishers was located – jotting down the biz plan en route.

The book store on the World Wide Web opened for business from their home, and in a few months the website was pulling in $20,000 in sales per week.

Amazon.com that Jeff founded was to become bigger than the river itself. Jeff's store was soon the World's Biggest store.

In a decade, Jeff Bezos was worth 8 billion.

******

CHAPTER 35
THE MARKET PLACE

The 1995 outbreak of Ebola virus killed over 200 people in Zaire. The death rate of those who contracted the disease was close to 80 percent. The entire world was gripped with fear of Ebola spreading.

Pam – Pierre's girlfriend – was a molecular biologist. She had always been fascinated by chemicals called enzymes, which catalyze biological reactions without being affected by the reactions themselves. She called them nature's activists.

Pierre and Pam knew the beauty of the chemistry of life. They also knew that a disease like Ebola could easily become a pandemic that could threaten humanity itself. They were community activists with a special interest in matters relating to health, life and pandemics.

They both understood the way life worked at the very fundamental levels. Cancer, pandemics, germs and viruses – all of these they noted, were processes that were not controlled by a central authority, but created by self-defining ecosystems.

Pierre collected loads of information on Ebola and added it to his homepage.

******

Pierre had also been working on a new idea for a simple website to conduct auctions, a simple way for *ecosystems of communities* to form and evolve – to buy and sell anything.

"The most fun buying and selling on the Web! Take part in an exciting auction, or put your own merchandise on auction, all free for buyers!" A simple note on a simple webpage said it all.

Pierre wanted to test the new auction site he had built. He looked around for something to sell and picked up a broken laser pointer.

In a few days, the bids for the laser pointer had reached up to $14.83.

******

Pierre knew it was a broken pointer. So he contacted the winning bidder and informed him that the laser pointer was broken.

"I want it. I am a collector of broken laser pointers," said the bidder.

Pierre had realized the power of the Internet.

He had realized that this new medium could bring every consumer of every taste to every seller with something to sell.

That was powerful indeed; such a marketplace had not existed anywhere.

******

Pierre's site would become eBay. The name eBay rhymed with Ebola, but that may have been pure coincidence.

eBay would viral out and conquer the inherent spirit and desire of humanity for a global marketplace and community.

Unlike the deadly Ebola virus that, luckily for humanity, did not spread during that fateful year.

Pierre Omidyar was 28 in 1995, when he launched his new site. In a decade, he was worth $5 billion.

******

CHAPTER 36
THE STREET

Bill, then just a kid, loved the microscope his parents had gifted him.

He loved seeing tiny creatures through the eyepiece.

But he hated his eyelashes which interfered with his vision and passion.

So he cut off his eyelashes.

Now he could see the tiny creatures better.

He would not let anything get in the way of what he wanted to do.

******

While tinkering with his Apple II in 1980, Bill had an idea. He envisioned a new way to buy and sell stocks from one's home, with a computer.

In two years, Bill Porter and his friend, Bernie Newcomb, devised a way to buy and sell stocks through a modem.

******

A dentist in Michigan made the first trade using their system on 11 July 1983.

Regan had just announced the Star Wars Initiative that would bring down the Soviet Union, and Microsoft was just getting ready to ship the first copy of Microsoft Word. And Bill was transforming the entire trading industry to a whole new paradigm.

Bill turned ticker tapes to streams of electrons. Trading from then on would be conducted at the speed of light.

******

Bill's company, eTrade, offered stock trading to AOL and Compuserve users in 1991.

eTrade switched to the World Wide Web early, and launched a new way for everyone to trade stocks, fueling the dot-com boom.

In 1996, eTrade went public, and the company was worth $8 billion by 1999.

******

CHAPTER 37
THE COMMERCE WEB

The World Wide Web had transformed from being a worldwide library (Web of Information, 1991-1995, The Web 0.0), to the web of commerce by 1994. Companies like Amazon, eBay and eTrade led the boom.

The new web was later called Web 1.0.

From 1995 to 2000, as the browser wars geared up, the web of commerce drove the markets to extraordinary heights.

******

With sky-high valuations, the gold rush was on in the Silicon Valley for half-a-decade, aided by lower interest rates and risk-ignoring investors.

'Get large fast, or get lost', 'Win the game of eyeballs', 'Mind share and Market Share', 'Spend now, profits later' – business models based on organic growth were irrelevant.

Billion-dollar valuations, for companies with not a penny in profits, became common place.

This golden era of dot-coms would die suddenly, shortly after 2000.

******

Direct access to the stock market, obtained through online brokers such as eTrade, created a new type of investors who cared little about risk. The common man, who was unaware of the tricks and intricacies of the market, was leading the gold rush. Even large companies took the opportunity to amass speculative investments.

A few real successes launched a million careless others and dot-com fever gripped the world. Every brick and mortar company needed to transform into a wire-and-machine company.

The market punished caution, and rewarded carelessness.

******

But soon things started to turn.

Dreams based on fantasy were soon shattered by a wiser market, without mercy. The boom was soon a bust.

******

And while the dot-com boom withered, the browser wars reached their most vicious phase.

******

CHAPTER 38
BROWSER WARS

"War is the father of everything," Heraclitus of Greece observed, in 500 BC.

******

The browser wars had started on 7 December 1995, when Bill Gates redirected the Microsoft juggernaut to become an Internet-focused company.

Netscape Navigator (from the nascent Netscape) and Internet Explorer (from the giant Microsoft) fought tooth and nail for years for dominance over ground that no one had tamed.

And the dot-com gold rush funneled investments of hundreds of millions into a web that was uncontrollably spreading its tentacles to every corner of the world.

******

The war spawned intense innovation.

Introduced by Netscape, Javascript came as a simple way to script the browser – to make changes dynamically after a page loaded.

141

CSS (Cascading Style Sheets) were an obvious extension to separate content from presentation. ASP (Active Server Pages from Microsoft) and J2EE (from Sun Microsystems) began powering the servers that powered the net. Web pages became organized into DOMs (Document Object Models). And HTML, the language of the web, woke up as Dynamic HTML (DHTML).

******

Microsoft's move into the web was critical in formulating the gigantic leaps in technology.

It already had deep access to the right pieces of software and technologies, which the fledgling Netscape did not have yet. Vector Graphics (VML – *Vector Markup Language*), Multi-Media (SMIL – *Synchronized Multi–media Integration Language*), Active Desktop (Integration of the web to the desktop), ActiveX (web components based on Microsoft Windows Technologies), and Active Channels (real-time feeds into the browser) – Microsoft blazed its way through.

Netscape was soon priced out of the market, as Microsoft gave their product free.

******

Microsoft was the second largest company in the world, after AIG, and Gates was clearly the richest man in the world.

On 18 May 1998, US Government attacked Microsoft.

The Most Powerful Country on the Planet
vs.
the Most Powerful Software Company on the Planet.

In the end, Microsoft was forced to untie its internet browser from its operating system. By tying things to the desktop, the courts ruled, Microsoft used its clear monopoly to the detriment of Netscape.

Though the government could shackle the giant, there was a bigger technical reason for the untying of the browser: the security risks that would plague Internet Explorer for years to come.

******

By November of 1998, Netscape was fading into history. It was sold to AOL for $4 billion.

******

Dot-com companies disappeared one after another. The world witnessed the horrors of 11 September 2001, followed by scandals at Enron, WorldCom and many others.

With a wiser market, Web 1.0 went silent.

Most thought it was over.

******

143

"The Internet is becoming the town square for the global village of tomorrow."

- Bill Gates,
Business @ the Speed of Thought,
15 May 2000

CHAPTER 39
WHEN THE MASSES MOVED

A few companies that had survived the big collapse of the commerce web and were by now smaller, leaner and meaner. A few innovators still had big ideas.

A company named Nupedia was formed in March 2000 to host encyclopedic information, supported by advertisements. By the end of November 2006, only two articles had been written using the system.

James Wales, founder of Nupedia, imagined a world *in which every single person on the planet can be given free access to the sum of all human knowledge.*

In January 2001, he launched his new idea: a website called Wikipedia.

wiki means fast in Hawaiian. Wikipedia was a peer-monitored system, protected in a cult-like fashion, yet which anyone could edit.

Nupedia was closed down in 2003 with only 100 articles ever written. But Wikipedia had mushroomed to 100,000 articles by 2003.

In another five years (2001–2005), articles in Wikipedia grew to 500,000.

It had 1 million articles by 2006. And in 2007, it crossed 2 million articles.

******

There was something compelling about the new concept of sharing knowledge, ideas and information across the world.

The free encyclopedia trounced existing commercial encyclopedias like the Encyclopedia Britannica, which was already under assault by Microsoft's Encarta.

******

With Wikipedia, the web was gradually taking the world's information and making it accessible and available to all – and the web was becoming a true repository of knowledge.

The new encyclopedia was the encyclopedia of the people, by the people, for the people.

******

While the knowledge revolution snowballed, another massive movement was occurring in how friends connected with each other and formed social constellations.

******

CHAPTER 40
A FACE THAT LAUNCHED A MILLION ACCOUNTS

Fall '03 seemed like yet another ordinary semester at Harvard.

Mark was upset with Jessica Alona. He had to find a way to get over her.

A bit drunk, Mark thought of an idea – a website to compare female students around the campus. He looked over the online facebook for Kirkland House, one of the many houses on campus, and wasn't sure if he liked all the faces he saw.

He thought of a voting system similar to 'hot or not': to compare and contrast people.

However, it was difficult to get pictures of all the students on campus. He decided to hack into the online directories of Harvard University.

Mark set up a simple website with information hacked from the online directories of nine (out of the twelve) Harvard houses. He named it www.facemash.com. Visitors could vote for the faces they liked, and the winner would be the one who got the highest votes.

He forwarded the email about www.facemash.com to a few friends. It was the last week of October, 2003.

******

Others sent the mail out over group list-servers on the campus. By 10 pm that day, 450 visitors had visited the site and voted 22,000 times for their favorites.

Some were not pleased, especially the groups for Latina and black students.

******

Mark was accused by Harvard University for breaching security, violating copyright and invading individual privacy – and for good reason. The Computer Services Department accused him with unauthorized use of the university's computing resources.

On 18 November 2003 the Administrative Board demanded Mark to appear before them to decide on the punishment.

Luckily for Mark Zuckerberg, the board decided not to expel him from the University.

******

But Mark had found his niche. He launched www.facebook.com on February 2004.

In four years, Facebook would mushroom to a social network of 175 million users, with $300 million in revenues, 700 employees and a valuation close to $15 billion.

******

Mark and Facebook were not the first ones, though. Social networking sites had started sprouting all over the globe, a couple of years before.

******

CHAPTER 41
THE PEOPLE NETWORK

When Jonathan Abrams founded Friendster in 2002, it was the very first online virtual community.

Friendster soon exploded into a phenomenon.

MySpace, LinkedIn and Facebook followed Friendster over the next two years.

News Corporation acquired MySpace in 2005 for $500 million.

While social networking sites were grabbing all the attention, people needed quick ways to embed pictures and videos into their social networking web pages.

flickr (a photo uploading site) and *YouTube* (a video uploading site) started giving free online storage to social networkers who were looking for storage space.

The growth of the storage sites was spectacular.

flickr, launched in February 2004, was acquired by Yahoo! for about $35 million in March 2005.

YouTube, launched by three former PayPal employees in February 2005 was mopped up by Google for a whopping $1.5 billion in November 2006.

******

While many found friendship and solace on the web, thousands of others were adopting a new way to express themselves to anyone who cared to listen.

This new media was mushrooming worldwide, shaking up the older, established media. Soon new bands of activists all over the world were making kings and paupers with their fingertips.

Finally the real power was in the hands of the people. Let us meet our voice next.

******

"You already have zero privacy – get over it."

> *– Scott McNealy,*
> *Former CEO of Sun Microsystems,*
> *25 January 1999*

CHAPTER 42
YOUR VOICE

A phenomenon called weblogs had started appearing in 1997, a replacement for UseNet Newsgroups using webpage technology.

By accident, a web-logger spelled the term weblog as *We Blog*. A new term blog had been coined.

******

Evan Williams and Meg Hourihan (Pyra Labs) launched blogger.com in August 1999 and popularized the term blog. Google acquired blogger in February 2003 in a secret deal.

******

The power of blogging was revealed by the role it played in exposing the fraudulent set of documents presented by CBS News anchor Dan Rather to discredit President Bush, during the 2004 Presidential Election.

On FreeRepublic.com website, on 8 September 2004, someone posted copies of the documents that were presented by CBS News relating to President Bush's National Guard service.

Shortly afterwards, someone named "BuckHead" suggested that the documents, called Killian documents (said to be made in the 70's), looked like forgeries.

It got the attention of the whole world. More and more people joined the research. Experts into 1970-era typewriters and printers poured in. Shortly after, drudgereport.com and powerlineblog.com joined the chorus.

Dr. Joseph Newcomer, a computer typography expert, stated on 15 September 2004 that it was impossible for the National Guard to have obtained laser printing technology, at the time the document was said to have been made.

The documents were proved to be forgeries, made using Microsoft Word. The event would shame CBS and end with the resignation of its anchor, Dan Rather.

******

Blogs also played a significant role in the downfall of Senator Trent Lott in December 2002.

Senator Lott had praised the past racist inclinations of Senator Strom Thurmond, at the old senator's 100th birthday party. Lott had said at the event: "When Strom Thurmond ran for president, we voted for him. We're proud of it. And if the rest of the country had followed our lead, we wouldn't have had all these problems over the years, either."

The statement may not have caught the attention of the mainstream media, but reverberated across the web – carried and echoed by bloggers. In fifteen days, Senator Lott would resign from the Senate Majority Leader position.

That was yet another example of *our* powerful voice.

******

Web was ushering in a new era of democracy: where everyone could speak and be heard.

Some observers took notice of the new democratic direction of the net – in blogs, in Wikipedia, in social networks and in other platforms.

The pundits were puzzled. These experts started theorizing on what they were observing and what to call this new web.

******

CHAPTER 43
THE SECOND GENERATION

Tim O'Reilly had been on the forefront of free software and open source movements. In 2001, he led the fight against Amazon's one click patent, widely seen as another ridiculous patent that would stifle innovation.

He and his team at O'Reilly Media noticed something rather interesting evolving on the web from the ashes of the dot-com bust. They tried to understand the differences between the old web and the new web, by writing them down on a whiteboard.

Tim noted that the web was evolving into a new kind of platform, one that harnessed collective intelligence and the wisdom of the crowds. This new generation of web was based on lightweight software that worked on any machine, created over much shorter release cycles.

On the left they marked Web 1.0, and on the right they coined a new term, Web 2.0.

The term Web 2.0 had come to define the web of community.

WWW was transforming to a new web.

It had become a *Constellation of Connected Communities*, a CCC.

******

"*What we really want to do at Google is to create AI.*"

- Larry Page,
Co-Founder of Google,
February 2004

CHAPTER 44
A BIT OF INFORMATION

In 2000, Microsoft introduced a technology called *Client-Side HTTP Access*, to enable their Outlook web-client to update status without refreshing the entire webpage. This became the cornerstone of AJAX (Asynchronized Javascript) that would later drive many new pieces of software on the Web.

******

Ajax was popularized by Google Maps and Meebo in 2005. Named by James Garrett, it became a popular technique, quickly absorbed by companies like Writely, Zoho, EditGrid, and many others in the coming years. There were alternatives to Ajax (such as techniques using iframes, available in Microsoft Internet Explorer since 1996), but they were not as elegant.

Ajax was one of the smoothest ways to implement refreshable controls on the web. It worked its way into many new portal designs, like Netvibes and iGoogle over the years. Microsoft Atlas also pushed Ajax designs into its development tools.

******

Web 2.0 was dominated by social networking and never-ending global conversations, far more than specific implementation techniques.

Throughout the world, conversation was no longer controlled by mainstream media. Anyone from anywhere in the world could command the world's attention, and hold it if needed.

Against the backdrop of the wars in Iraq and Afghanistan, individuals were reporting to a world eager to hear unfiltered stories.

In the First Gulf War, CNN had presented the world with the Iraqi side of the story, but in the Second Gulf War, blogs and amateur reports drove the world's opinion – much like the ham-radios of decades past.

Even terrorists took best use of the web as a medium to spread hatred and to organize their evil operations. The good guys needed to update themselves to new ways, in which the web-world worked.

******

In March of 2006, a company named Twitter was launched with a 140 character SMS service. The service, a brainchild of Jack Dorsey, was promoted by Evan Williams who had previously sold blogger.com to Google.

Jack had been working on emergency services software, and knew the importance of real-time communication. He drew up an idea to connect friends using a messaging service in July 2000, and started working on it seriously in 2006.

Today there are over a hundred Twitter look-alikes around the world. And perpetually connected streams of short-messages have evolved to become an integral part of our thought process like email.

******

Since Twitter could work with any type of device (like cell phones), people have been finding interesting and unexpected uses for the service.

When terrorists ran amuck in Mumbai, Twitter was chirping 15 times a second with real-time updates on every aspect of the unfolding drama.

The Twitter story showcases how humans devise simple solutions to solve complicated problems with a bit of ingenuity and good sense.

******

The Constellation of Connected Communities (Web 2.0) created a new way for the world to think, write, connect and socialize. Then one of Tim Berners-Lee's dormant dreams started to rear its head again in 2006.

******

CHAPTER 45
THE THIRD GENERATION

Victor Shannon wrote an article titled "A 'more revolutionary' Web" in International Herald Tribune on 24 May 2006 that stated: "Just when the ideas behind 'Web 2.0' are starting to enter the mainstream, the brains behind the World Wide Web are introducing pieces of what may end up being called Web 3.0."

Victor was quoting Tim Berners-Lee, who was addressing the 15th annual International World Wide Web Conference the day before.

"The Web is only going to get more revolutionary," Tim said.

"People keep asking what Web 3.0 is," Tim continued. "I think maybe when you've got an overlay of scalable vector graphics – everything rippling and folding and looking misty – on Web 2.0 and access to a semantic web integrated across a huge space of data, you'll have access to an unbelievable data resource."

******

In his landmark New York Times article printed on 12 November 2006, "Entrepreneurs See a Web Guided by Common Sense," John Markoff introduced a new term to the American mainstream.

"From the billions of documents that form the World Wide Web and the links that weave them together, computer scientists and a growing collection of start-up companies are finding new ways to mine human intelligence. Their goal is to add a layer of meaning on top of the existing Web that would make it less of a catalog and more of a guide — and even provide the foundation for systems that can reason in a human fashion. That level of artificial intelligence, with machines doing the thinking instead of simply following commands, has eluded researchers for more than half a century. Referred to as Web 3.0, the effort is in its infancy, and the very idea has given rise to skeptics who have called it an unobtainable vision."

John Markoff was introducing a new generation of the web to the world.

******

Nova Spivack expanded the idea on 17 December 2006.

He wrote, "The threshold to the third-generation web will be crossed in 2007. At this juncture the focus of innovation will start to shift back from front-end improvements towards back-end infrastructure level upgrades to the web. This cycle will continue for five

163

to ten years, and will result in making the web more connected, more open, and more intelligent. It will transform the web from a network of separately siloed applications and content repositories to a more seamless and interoperable whole."

******

The observations by John and Nova portrayed the slow fading away of the Web of Community or Web 2.0 and the transition to a Semantic Omni-Functional Web, Web 3.0.

They were pointing at a web of data enriched with a web of functionality.

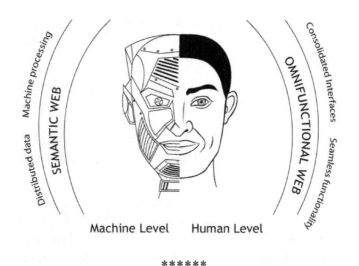

Machine Level   Human Level

******

CHAPTER 46
THE GGG

In the beginning there were computers. Then networks were created for the machines to talk to each other.

Tim then created the WWW, where he linked pages to other pages in a World Wide Web.

He looked at his creation and he was not happy.

He noted: The net linked computers, whereas the web linked documents.

He lamented that the web was two-dimensional, kind of.

On 21 November 2007 he created a new concept and posted it on his blog. He called it the Giant Global Graph, or the GGG.

******

Graph is a loaded term. In the world of mathematics, graph means a set of objects where some pairs of objects are connected by links. It is a set of vertices, connected by lines (or curves) called edges.

Like dots, connected by lines crisscrossing in between.

Tim was imagining a web that would connect data, ideas, and concepts in a universe called the semantic web.

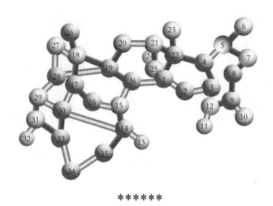

******

Let us try to put this in perspective.

I have an ID (maybe a Social Security Number, 345-30-3330, which may no longer be a secret number in a few more years!). I am going to New York. I am taking Continental flight 89 from Houston IAH to Newark EWR on 5 March 2015. My return trip is from Washington DCA to Houston IAH on 8 March 2015 by Continental flight 159. My meeting with a venture capitalist, Elisa at Smart Guys Capital, is at 8:00 am on 6 March 2015.

Elisa has a medical appointment on 7 March 2015. But it is moved to 6 March 2015, due to some unforeseen changes in her health. She goes to hospital in the wee hours of the morning.

GGG is watching and knows my trip needs to be rescheduled.

Now look at the systems. Continental's flight system knows my plan. Imagine that my ID is connected to the airline data, as well as the scheduling data for Elisa.

In the semantic web, data is connected through appropriate metadata (data about data itself) so that these connections can be established, and therefore decisions can be made quickly and effectively.

The GGG informs me of the change in plans and suggests rescheduling my trip. I reschedule to make better use of my time.

Maybe GGG may even order and download the new book written by my favorite author (which GGG knew was going to be released on that day), to fill the extra time.

******

The OLIVER that Lick had predicted in 1965 would come to life in the GGG.

The GGG may manage us in the future. There may be a time when the web becomes the embodiment of what we think of as humanity. The billions of displays, cell phones, cars, homes, offices, desktops, all connected to a cloud of computation – a single machine in concept. All displays become just windows to a virtual world that we live in.

If we misbehave, our account is deactivated by the GGG, and we cease to exist or "live" in the "real" world.

GGG may become the soul of humanity. Maybe even a God in concept that knows all and controls everything. We may become just spiders on a web. Anything and everything we think and make, becomes a piece of this global mechanism.

It is not far-fetched.

******

All other media are already converging into the web: thoughts, audio-video, phones, chats, films, books, emails, songs, pictures, maps, websites, papers, documents, feelings, designs, desires, catalogues … in fact, everything.

But so far these have been in islands of data, housed in different sites and locations, not really connected. The web has large constellations of data, with no clear connections that may be meaningful to machines.

******

Now imagine new devices – possibly based on nanotechnology – that can extend their silicon hands to embrace every part of our lives. Imagine chips in our refrigerators, cars, clothes, curtains and homes. Everything we own and know – that web-aware

Mercedes and that web-aware mansion in Southern California, tracked and seen by anyone who cares.

We live in a world that already knows your address, has a high-resolution picture of your house (in three-dimensions in the near future), on street maps, for anyone who cares to see.

Even your transient thoughts, your chatter and your mails, are etched into the permanent, unforgiving memory of the GGG.

A web that can give you every picture taken by anyone, sorted by date and tags.

A web that knows all your relationships, even proposed ones. A web that knows every one for whom you have ever searched, and who ever who have searched for you.

A web where "ex" is not a term, but another GGG id that refuses to go away.

Now imagine the semantic web that connects them all – with the overarching logic to glue it all together. A graph with connectors that would auto-link related information, though no one ever designed those links specifically.

It is a web where you find friends just because you are lucky (or unlucky) enough to have been connected by a machine somehow. You meet someone on the electronic bulletin-board, rather than your own neighborhood.

Imagine life with thinking things that are able to discover connections and make decisions without any central control.

Billions of eyes that see you and billions of ears that listen to you.

Not just when you were there, nor just when you were speaking.

But forever!

It's not just scary; that is the world we are already living in.

******

In the 50s, how fast you could do mental math was important. Now no one cares. Computers can do it better.

In the 70s how fast you could think was important. Now no one cares. Computers can do it faster.

In the 90s, how much you knew was important. What books you had read, and what newspaper you read daily was important.

Now no one cares. The web can do it better.

Already the web knows better.

It can search better.

It has more information than you have ever had, or will ever have.

******

170

The GGG is the soul of humanity.

That is, until the next revolution.

The revolution when the web starts to generate and find new knowledge.

When the web makes connections that create new information; working at the speeds of light, not at the slow pace of the inaccurate chemical brain.

The revolution of the *Intelligent Immersive Imagion*.

Let us think of Imagion as a *machine with imagination*.

Not a robot, but a soul with eyes and ears numbering into the billions and billions. A being that can feel us, knows us, and defines us.

Let us call that the III.

III, a tribute to I, U (You) and V (We) becoming one with the machine.

Respectfully we will yield the stage to the machine.

And the *Age of Imagion* will be on.

******

171

"People always fear change. People feared electricity when it was invented, didn't they? People feared coal, they feared gas-powered engines ... There will always be ignorance, and ignorance leads to fear. But with time, people will come to accept their silicon masters."

—*Bill Gates,*
CEO Microsoft,
2000

CHAPTER 47
THE INKLESS PRESS

Johannes Gutenberg, a goldsmith, combined the idea of a press (used to flatten olives and grapes) with the idea of 'movable types', which he made out of tin, lead and antimony – and launched a revolution in 1453.

The printing revolution would evolve into the Renaissance that paved the way for our way of life today.

Yet, it was not Gutenberg who generated the real revolution of enlightenment. His books were bulky and difficult to carry around. It was not his fault really; he was only trying to be compatible with the manuscripts of huge sizes of those days, just so that people adopted his works easily.

******

By 1482, the printing capital of the world was Venice, not Germany, and the leading press was Aldine Press, run by Aldus Manutis.

Aldus loved the Greek classics, and he wanted everyone else to enjoy them too. He realized that if he reduced the size of the books to something people could easily carry around, many more people would be able to read them.

He set his goal on books the size of a saddle bag – about the size of a paperback today. He folded the standard paper into eight, and made books of the *octavo* size, called the Aldine editions.

The right form factor made all the difference. His books spread like wild fire throughout the land, making knowledge accessible to everyone.

******

Aldus was a true genius. He transformed books into their current design and format, complete with table

174

of contents, pages, indexes, etc.

He, along with his son, created the *italic* fonts and punctuations. They invented the semi-colon (;), started using periods (.) and colons (:) to end sentences, and created the symbol for comma (,). A comma was literally a lowered forward slash (the virgule, '/').

Aldus literally converted printing into a revolution that sparked a million minds.

******

Aldus PageMaker software was named after Aldus Manutis of Venice.

PageMaker, made by Aldus Corporation, launched the DTP (*D*esk*t*op *P*ublishing) industry, which made Apple Macintosh computer so popular.

Aldus Corporation was the creator of TIFF, a popular graphics format. It also created Freehand, a vector drawing program that eventually morphed into Macromedia Flash. Aldus Corporation was later bought by Adobe.

Three Aldus programmers founded Visio Corporation, which later became Microsoft Visio, in a $1.5 billion deal.

Adobe later purchased Macromedia for $4 billion.

Aldus from Venice still reverberates through many leading software companies of today.

******

175

Tim Berners-Lee launched an inkless printing press revolution in 1991. And Marc Andreessen, the creator of Mosaic and Netscape, carried on the revolution to a commercial product.

Marc, in an article on 8 January 1999 called a soft-spoken 35-year-old from a remote village of Trichy, India, as the "Aldus of the Net."

Aldus is a remarkable figure; so how did Ramanathan V. Guha become the Aldus of the Internet?

******

CHAPTER 48
THE ALDUS OF THE WEB

In 1986, Guha (a mechanical engineer from IIT Madras) was doing his master's in Mechanical Engineering at the University of California, Berkeley. During his studies he came across a subject called artificial intelligence (AI). He was so fascinated by it that he sent his resume to MCC, a research company that was creating *Cyc*, a commonsense knowledge base for AI.

MCC called Guha back to reject his application, very politely.

"Well, we really don't have the room. We already have all of our students that we need," the caller said.

"Okay, no problem. I'll work at night," Guha replied.

"But we don't have an office for you," the caller responded.

"That's okay, I'll work wherever," Guha was persistent.

Guha was hired by MCC.

In three weeks Guha was given his own office, and MCC wanted Guha to stay.

And Guha did, for seven-and-a-half years.

******

Guha realized that AI was in its infancy. The real problem was not that computers couldn't do advanced things, but that they could not do most of the silly things humans took for granted.

Later, Guha moved on to Apple, where he developed something called the Meta Content Framework (MCF). MCF was a way to represent *metadata* (or information about information) that could fill in the gaps in information flow among disparate software products.

When Steve Jobs returned to Apple, the company started to cut back on research. Guha soon left Apple, for Netscape.

At Netscape, he met Tim Bray, someone who had been defining what was called XML.

******

XML (Extended Markup Language), a variant of SGML, is a language to markup data.

If data stored in a file had only data, no one will be able to use it unless the structure of the file was described or known in some other way. Marking up data helped describe areas of data with more details so anyone (including a machine) could comprehend it and use it. Bulky, yet flexible and powerful, XML is the language of the semantic web.

Example of XML

```
<?xml version="1.0" encoding="UTF-8" ?>
<animal name="dog" lifespan="14 years">
        <title>Dog</title>
        <food>
                <item>Water</item>
                <item>Dog Food</item>
        </food>
</animal>
```

******

XML is simply data with markup. A machine or a person can read the data given in XML with simple parsing, and use it to do other things.

Tim and Guha combined their ideas of XML and MCF, and the Resource Description Framework (RDF) was born.

Guha later used RDF in March 1999 at the my.netscape.com portal as the *RDF Site Summary* (RSS). Netscape was by then a part of AOL.

Later, others simplified the RSS format and renamed it as 'Really Simple Syndication'. Today, most news sites provide RSS feeds of their news, and RSS is considered one of the most popular XML formats.

The real significance of RDF is in the world of semantic web, which is explained in more detail in Appendix 1: Semantic Technology.

Guha, through his pioneering work, was defining the metadata of the semantic web. He was actually paving the way for the next generation of the Internet.

The Aldus of the Web was reformatting the revolution itself.

******

Over the coming decades, web will transform into a more pervasive phenomenon that envelopes us all, just like air and electricity!

So let us consider the generational transformations that have been happening on this medium called the Web, so that we may foresee our own future.

******

"I have a dream for the web [in which computers] become capable of analyzing all the data on the web – the content, links, and transactions between people and computers. A 'Semantic Web', which should make this possible, has yet to emerge, but when it does, the day-to-day mechanisms of trade, bureaucracy and our daily lives will be handled by machines talking to machines. The 'intelligent agents' people have touted for ages will finally materialize."

- *Tim Berners-Lee,*
Weaving the Web: Origins and Future of the World Wide Web,
1999

CHAPTER 49
WEB GENERATIONS

The evolution from WWW to CCC to GGG to III demonstrates a fascinating extension of human creativity into the realm of information, knowledge, functionality and relationships.

It took a human lifetime for information to circumnavigate the earth, just a few hundred years ago. Now information reaches all corners of the globe in seconds.

We are now living in a world that works on instantaneous information and sub-second decisions. Our society has been transforming in fundamental ways, because of a web that has been evolving rapidly in power and nature. With the cumulative growth of network and hardware capacity, the newer generations of the web will define our future.

******

The evolution of the GGG, the third generation, covers two aspects: the web of data and the web of functionality, as we shall see next.

******

Generations of the Web

WWW	1991-1996	Web 0.0 Information Web ***Library of Information***
	1997-2002	Web 1.0 Commerce Web ***World Wide Web***
CCC	2001-2007	Web 2.0 Community Web ***Constellations of Connected Communities***
GGG	2006-2011	Web 3.0 Semantic Web/Omni-Functional Web ***Giant Global Graph***
III	2011-2015 2014-2020 2020-2025	Web 3.2 - Immersive Web Web 3.5 - Learning Web Web 4.0 - Knowledge Web ***Intelligent Immersive Imagion***

******

CHAPTER 50
WEB OF DATA

Data is everywhere. However, useful data requires more data about data itself, or metadata.

A following sentence (or data) does not make any sense by itself:
"TBL, 2000 Web Street, London, UK"

But if provided with more metadata that describes the data better, the information may become useful.

For example, if it is specified that the first field contains a name, the second field contains a street address, the third field contains a city, and the fourth field contains a country, then it could be concluded that the data is an address. Such metadata is required to effectively understand and use data.

******

In practice, the need to search within data can range from recovery to reasoning.

At the very basic level, data in simple text or comma separated formats can be used to recover only facts, not to discover new information.

As the amount of metadata increases, as in relational databases, systems can be designed to discover and identify new facts.

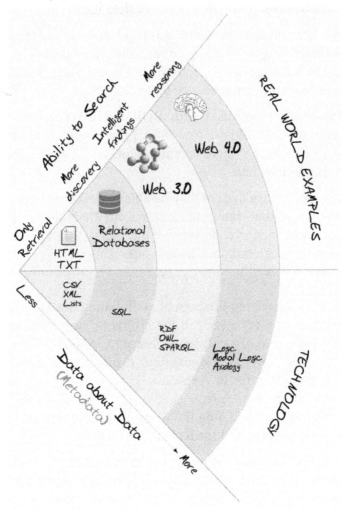

For example, SQL can be used to query a database to figure out the youngest or the oldest employee. This is possible due to the increased metadata in the database describing the employee data itself.

As the amount of metadata is increased, we can actually find new intelligent facts out of the data. This is the realm of data spectrum (in the last figure) that embraces the semantic web technology.

Information provided with RDF and OWL (please refer to *Appendix 1: Semantic Technologies* for on this) can enable more intelligent decisions based on the available data.

For example, a system may be able to find employees having similar interests, and inform them about a particular activity of interest to them; all without intentional preordained human intervention.

******

A very interesting offshoot of assimilating the data on the web can been seen in the efforts of sites such as *www.dbpedia.org*, *freebase*, *Semantic MediaWiki* and the *W3C SWEO Community Project* (For more information refer to Appendix 2: Data Web). These sites attempt to create a World Wide Database (*WWDB*) consolidating the world's information from sources such as Wikipedia and other sites.

It is notable that DBpedia works by extracting data from Wikipedia pages. For example, the Wikipedia page on France contains an InfoBox that gives information about France in a standard way in a table on the top right.

DBpedia cleverly uses this information to populate its data web, which then can be queried using SPARQL (*SPARQL Protocol and RDF Query Language*), a semantic querying language, using tools available over the web.

Now DBpedia also links to other data sources like CIA Factbook, Quotations Book, US Census Data, flickr, Geonames, Wordnet, Google Maps, and several other databases.

By 2008, DBpedia had detailed data on about three million things and 300 million facts. All that information can be queried using the next generation of web enabled tools.

******

The next level of search capability goes into the realm of reasoning.

With first order logic, systems can start to reason. And with modal logic, systems may be able to think in approximations, like the human brain. With reasoning supported by *trust*, *proof* and *verifiability*, the process can become more reliable, and people can start to depend on its conclusions. This is possibly the dawn of an ultimate reasoning tool.

******

GPS devices less than the size of a credit card, can do a better job already than most humans in dynamic route determination. As more live data can be fed into such systems regarding traffic, construction work, etc. these devices may be able to do even better. For example, these devices may be able to get real-time information from traffic control devices (like traffic signals), which may allow for better traffic management, and even automatic vehicle control (without human drivers) may become possible using this technology.

At this time, much of the higher-end semantic web is theoretical in nature – especially in concept formation, problem solving and decision-making. Yet, there is still value in approximate answers that can free up more time for the human brain to do better things, like finding, organizing and solving things faster.

At the moment, Google has become the Oracle of everything, and the next generation search mechanisms may provide even more intelligent results which are personalized and smarter – that the mechanism may anticipate the question itself!

******

The availability of immense amounts of data clearly will open up tremendous possibilities. However, the other significant step forward will be the ability to do whatever you want with the data. That brings us to a concept called *Omni-Functionality*, the ability to do anything and everything!

******

CHAPTER 51
IDEA + SQUARE = ORIGAMI

Robert Lang, an expert at the ancient Japanese art of paper folding, explained the art as:

Idea + Square = Origami

******

On 17 February 2006, in a remote office in Houston, a new website was created with a novel technology called GAMI. It was the short form for '*Go Ahead. Move It!*', which was a technology invented by sheer accident!

It was just a way to make all objects on a webpage to move. It was done in a totally new and simple manner, yet in a strange way. It was a very low profile development.

In March 2006, GAMI was used to create a primitive technology called a recursive browser. Again, nothing unusual was noticeable, except that it looked very ugly and crude, yet there was something cool about it.

The simple development then started to take an unexpected turn. The developers theorized many things, but were still not sure what it all meant.

By April 2006, the simple structure had started showing some strange, yet powerful properties. The team theorized that it could result in interesting ways to contain objects within data structures that could represent metadata of unusual nature.

For example, an image in the platform could be addressed from another page in a standard way. Or even contain an image inside another image. It looked very recursive in nature.

First named Notes, it was soon renamed Cubes.

In weeks, the cubes and the weird idea had mushroomed into something big. A simple page could now be a container of any structure. Each part of the page could become a drawing, a video, an image, a conversation, a song, a program, a note, a poem, a webpage, an island of data – anything that users wanted it to be.

GAMI became ORI-GAMI, just like paper folds that transforms into beautiful objects.

An Idea + Cubes = ORI-GAMI.

A three dimensional world of unusual power was emerging out of simple HTML and Javascript. The simple page was transforming into a massive universe of power hitherto unknown.

******

190

What happened in those spring nights became clear a few months later. The platform made pages into editable documents. The documents could then transform to become programs. Programs could then become environments. Environments became platforms. Platforms became a world. A world would become a page again. Or it could take any form that it chose.

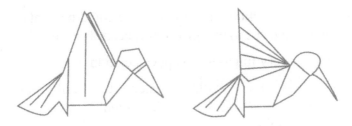

The bottom line was that the user decided what functions he needed than the programmer deciding what functions needed to be programmed. All of this was very unusual.

It did not matter what the user wanted to do, the platform transformed to what was needed. All by itself!

What occurred was later recognized as *omni-functionality* - an emergent behavior that made possible whatever the user desired.

******

Modern age computers differentiated themselves from earlier machines by the fact that they were freely programmable devices and could take any function at will. They had become omni-functional hardware.

However, software had never been that way. It was always custom made for a specific function or a set of predetermined functions.

Omni-functionality software was a paradigm shift.

******

In Cubes, functionalities of any type could be applied in any sequence to any group of objects as desired.

That is, every function except calculation.

For that the world needed to wait until 1 September 2007, for the invention of something called CALCI.

CALCI was a way to turn a webpage into a more powerful calculation medium than any known thus far; a webpage many times more flexible and powerful that any known spreadsheets or calculators. In ways that were thought practically impossible before.

Now the platform could do things in ways that a page was never even expected to do.

******

Imagine a page that can calculate in ways that surpass *Excel*, paint a Mona Lisa with its beautiful smile, make a slide show shaped like a butterfly, and browse in ways so unusual that would put a browser to shame. What had been invented was a Recursive

Browser of power never seen before. No program had ever done so much, even if intentionally designed.

By 2008, ORI-GAMI would become a communication platform with blogs, walls, email and an ultra-powerful search.

Everything, though, was still just a browser page. A simple browser page took the shape that was needed when it was needed.

That was all! But it could do it all!

******

Omni-functionality is no longer a vague concept.

It is what users had always wanted.

So far, programs had been developed with known set of objectives by custom design – always with fixed set of functionalities.

That constrained users to do just what the *designers wanted the users to do*.

******

With the new idea of ZCubes – its new name – the user was in control of *whatever* the user wanted, *whenever* the user wanted, and *however* the user wanted.

With equal ease of putting a smile on Mona Lisa, a novice could watch movies and calculate the Fibonacci series, project loan payments and add up complex numbers. All the while browsing, or handwriting, or rotating a picture in three dimensions with no particular sequence in mind.

The user could do things that he or she actually had no reason even to think of.

******

Thinking mechanized. Thoughts freed.

Like a freely programmable device, the new omni-functional software freely transformed into anything that the users wanted the software to be.

Omni-functionality is bound to revolutionize the way we think about computing.

******

On 28 May 2009, Google announced a new technology called Google Wave. This open protocol, like the email protocols of the past, is a precursor of how function-agnostic thinking may revolutionize how we communicate.

Waves are essentially threads of conversations built by users (similar to Cubees and Channels in ZCubes). For example, a user can add a message to another message, by inserting it *into* the conversation text by just clicking on the word and adding it.

Imagine threads of conversations, pointing exactly to the specific point of interest in the text. The implications are enormous. Waves make emails, blogs, instant conversations, twittered messages, etc. come into a single thread of conversation, as in a tree

194

of information, just the way we think. The Wave system makes collaboration easy, and works beautifully for both synchronous and asynchronous communication, and can even track the history of the conversation.

A powerful enhancement to Google Waves are robots that reside on the server, which may specialize on tasks like spell checking, grammar checking, translation, task management, polls, forms, question-answers, etc. It can safely be said that the days of the OLIVER (that JCR Licklider envisioned) are almost here. By treating Waves as documents of informal nature, one can visualize very effective ways of managing workflow.

The notable aspect of the Google Wave effort is that it is open in nature. The supporting machines may reside not just in Google servers, but also enterprises and other providers, making it possible to have Waves work just like email someday.

Threads of thought are captured, distributed, shared, modified, and managed easily through this fascinating platform. Google Waves essentially makes threads conversations into a URL (similar to Cubees), which falls back to the basic design of the internet. An amazing technology that is bound to revolutionize communication and collaboration, it shows another example of the transition of the web to an omni-functional function-agnostic world.

******

Amazon Kindle was a mono-functional device that was released by Amazon in November 2007, to aid reading of eBooks. With increasing power of omni-functional cell-phones, a merging of devices like Kindle into the mobile platform can easily be foreseen.

******

Technologies like ZCubes (specializing in functionality), Mobile devices (specializing in connectivity, constant user engagement and local-specific services) and Google Waves (specializing in communication and collaboration), will continue to blur the need to think about separate applications, and let users express and communicate in fascinatingly powerful ways.

Newer mobile technologies may provide the ability and bandwidth that allow any functionality to be delivered to any platform that can compute.

Imagine a cell phone that is also a credit card, driver's license, passport, GPS, garage-door-opener, radio, TV, iPod, portfolio manager and constant companion; yet more powerful than a current desktop PC. Such devices with constant connectivity and omni-functionality may make us think very differently about computing itself.

Computing and connectivity may soon become a natural part of our life.

******

It can be expected that hybrids of such technologies as described above, which use combinations of powerful web clients and massively scalable server architectures will completely transform the way we think, learn and compute, in the years to come!

******

As we head into a new future, there are some very strange and powerful techniques on the computing horizon. Let us take a look at some of these new computing architectures next.

These techniques are fast, powerful, absolutely unconventional and totally mind-boggling.

******

CHAPTER 52
UNCONVENTIONAL
COMPUTING

The von-Neumann architecture of computer hardware has ruled since the middle of the 20th century. And digital devices dominate the industry.

But digital computing based on binary numbering systems may soon be challenged by a series of novel techniques. Such unusual architectures and methods are collectively called *Unconventional Computing*.

Let us look at some examples.

Optical Computers that use photons (instead of electrons) may result in computing devices 10 times faster than that of electronic computers (since electricity travels at roughly 10 percent of the speed of light).

Chemical Computers may use concentrations of chemicals in clustered media to represent data and algorithms, like the brain itself. These massively parallel techniques may be very useful in domains like image processing.

Natural Computers may derive inspiration from biological processes like evolution, genetics, neural networks, immune systems, and swarm intelligence. Each of these may provide elegant solutions to specific problem domains.

For example, swarm intelligence may be applicable in areas where *a global intelligence* pervades groups constituted by simpler organisms behaving in a self-organized manner. Or immune system behavior (with memory of past diseases) may inspire computational techniques that recognize patterns and react.

Such techniques may provide the possibility of emergent behavior, where a system exhibits unexpected characteristics and behavior, not originally designed for or expected from the individual components. Nature's proven techniques may supply solutions and architectures that rigid sequential silicon designs may never provide – especially in problem areas where such approaches are a natural fit.

Quantum Computers use qubits instead of bits. Qubits are like bits, but with a probability attached to the elements 0 and 1, meaning that the value ψ stored in a qubit is: $\psi = \alpha * |0| + \beta * |1|$. Thus, a qubit can represent a value *somewhere in between 0 and 1*, unlike the rigid 0 and 1 in a conventional binary computer. This can result in compact computers, better information processing and storage in the future.

It is expected that silicon chip designs will run against molecular level constraints after 2015, according to Moore's Law, which predicts that the number of transistors possible in integrated circuits will double every two years.

Hopefully by then (2015, which is only five years away!) computer architectures may have shifted to quantum and/or optical designs.

Some of the techniques and unconventional ways of thinking just described, may give rise to a variety of future applications and fascinating machines.

******

Let us try to understand some of these by looking at how nature itself works at its core.

Let us look at the beautiful algorithm of nature itself.

******

"Clouds are not spheres, mountains are not cones, coastlines are not circles, and bark is not smooth, nor does lightning travel in a straight line."

— *Benoît Mandelbrot,*
in his introduction to
The Fractal Geometry of Nature,
1982

CHAPTER 53
THE BEAUTY OF FRACTALS

The War to End All Wars, otherwise known as World War I, killed about 16 million people during 1914-1918. The Spanish Flu that followed the war (from 1918 to 1920) killed somewhere between 20 to 100 million people.

Benoît's mother was a doctor. She had seen the ravage of the Spanish Flu, and she wanted to keep her son away from epidemics often seen in the cities.

The intense poverty and the deep desire to stay out of the cities resulted in Benoît being taught by his uncle, who was both a mathematician and a painter. Benoît would eventually combine the math he learned with art, to explain much of the world around us.

******

Benoît was always pulled towards the idea of roughness.

Scientists had long depended on techniques like Root-Mean-Square, which explained roughness in scientific terms as "a mean value and mild variations from that (or errors)."

That bothered Benoît.

He studied geometric patterns of galaxies, shape of metal fractures, earth's contours and coastlines for insights. None of them fit into 'the mean value and mild variation' concept that scientists were in love with.

Instead, Benoît imagined an idea in which small things could gave rise to cumulative patterns on repeated application.

For example, in a tree, branches divided into many, and then many more, and more, until the leaves sprouted out; thus forming the entire tree. He coined the term 'self-similar patterns' to refer to the repeated application of patterns that resulted in a final form.

He saw galaxies ballooning out of cloud clusters, one upon other; coastlines not as straight lines, but similar patterns one upon another; even stock prices as a pattern of repeated elemental moves.

Even turbulence of flows was better explained by Benoît's concepts of wild variability from basic patterns and randomness. His concepts worked far better than other theories on turbulence thus far.

He called the way the world worked as *fractals*.

******

A living-being is made of self-organized repeated duplication of cells. The branches of a tree divides repeatedly to form beautiful patterns. A cauliflower bunch forms out of tinier branches.

203

So many things in the natural world, that are driven by simple phenomena, can be explained by Benoît's fractals.

It is actually easy to understand.

Fractal Theory suggested that many things can be explained as composed of particles and structures that are more detailed than its final form – generated by the repeated application of some fundamental pattern.

For example, a financial transaction between two people, then between two entities, and then between two larger entities, results in what is called an *economy*. Elemental particles self-organize into crystals that eventually form a shape, which may otherwise be dismissed as rough. Even the behavior of society can be traced back to the interactions of human beings over and over again – eventually creating a social structure, or even cultures.

******

Benoît first used the term *fractal* in 1975, the same year Bill Gates founded Microsoft in New Mexico. Benoît had access to powerful computers to test his theory at IBM, which involved large amounts of computation intensive work. The fractal pictures that were generated out of the powerful computers gave him insights at levels impossible to match with any other technique before.

******

Fractals may be used to understand observations that defy simple explanations at first, but which are derived from simpler things within. Once you find the simpler detail, the complexity at the surface suddenly gives way to simple beauty and easy understanding.

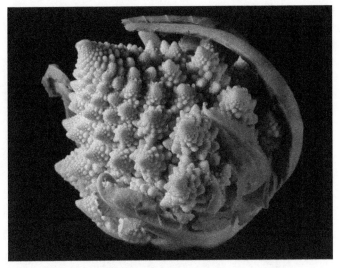

Fractals in Nature: Romanesco broccoli
(Photo courtesy PDPhoto.org)

******

Benoît Mandelbrot had found so much using a single concept. He had a magic formula that explained the shape of clouds, galaxies, continents, trees, leaves, creatures, feathers, brain and crystals.

From normal growth of cells to abnormal growth of cells (cancer); from spreading of offspring of a tree across a rainforest to branches of the same tree; from spreading of epidemics to spread of a virus in an animal – everything that was seeded from one fundamental concept could be explained by fractals.

Benoît had something that could explain trends in the stock market, from macroeconomics to micro-credit, from social structures to massive organizations, and so much more.

The world has finally started to realize that the Gaussian Distribution-based theory that has driven our decision-making for centuries has to be replaced by a more applicable Mandelbrot Distribution. In fact, Nassem Taleb, author of *The Black Swan*, based his entire economic theory on the power of Benoît's fractals.

Fractals can even explain the formation of networks of communities and ecosystems. It may someday even explain the transformation of the web into a 'being' that would at some point be composed of self-similar computing units that are networked – like a human brain with several million folds and connections.

******

Fractals became prominent because of the power of computers. Likewise, in the future, fractals may power many of our algorithms and analysis.

Fractals explain the way much of the real world works. There is so much to learn from the most beautiful and divine algorithm of all. The algorithm of life; that is also based on fractals. That is next.

******

CHAPTER 54
BITS OF CODE

The US Library of Congress is the largest library of information and books in the world.

A single genomics company today spits out more data than the entire US Library of Congress, every month!

The bits of code that drive life are being deciphered as fast as the human race and its machines can read them.

******

Life is recorded in five letters: A, T, C, G, and then U.

Adenine (A) and Thymine (T).

Cytosine (C) and Guanine (G).

In DNA, A will pair with T, and C will pair with G. This pairing assists in keeping the accuracy of the code during replication and transcription.

Thymine (T) found in DNA may be replaced by Uracil (U) in RNA.

These letters encode all of life. Just like the 0 and 1 in digital machines.

******

But there is a huge difference. Life is a recursive, self-sustaining, reproducing, evolving paradigm created by supernatural logic.

The digital mind is still a crude simulation of the human brain, attempting to mechanize some of what we want to and can.

******

Every living-being on the planet runs on a code of four letters. Grass, wheat, rice, meat, milk, plants, animals, hair, nails, dog, cat, snail, fish, flowers and wood – all emerge out of this basic secret code.

Almost everything we see and many things we cannot see are driven by a simple encoding of the four nucleobases in infinite patterns, which is then coiled and coiled and coiled and coiled into chromosomes.

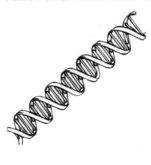

The color of our eyes and skin, our height and our emotional nature, are all controlled by the unseen bits of code – the DNA. And yes, four letters code the brain, which drives our intelligence.

The code taken equally from man and woman makes a child; the algorithm of life makes new life.

******

The computer of life is within cells, each of which has captured the primordial soup forever.

Dividing, multiplying, and evolving with only one intent – to keep life running.

How does the beautiful and intricate natural code form a *being* that spans the globe? That takes us to Gaia.

******

CHAPTER 55
THE LOGIC OF LIFE

Life, as we know it, exists only on earth.

James Lovelock, a student of life and a professor of sciences, first proposed the Gaia Hypothesis. The Gaia concept (named after the Greek Goddess of earth) views earth as a single organism powered by life, which regulates its internal environment so as to maintain a stable, constant state (homeostatic balance). Life is the soul of Gaia, a bio-geo-chemical process which permeates a thin layer of the earth and the sky. All in a thin layer – as thin as a paper wrap over a beach ball.

******

The code of life, written and rewritten by the hands of God or other divine entity, drives all of life. Every genetic code is expressed in triplets called codons, which are groups of any three of A, G, C, T combinations (e.g., ACC, GGC, TCA, etc.).

Each codon represents an amino acid. So each series of codons represent a series of amino acids, which combine to form a protein (a concatenated amino acid sequence). Though there could be 64 (4^3) amino acids

211

represented by the triplet codons of four letters, only about 20 amino acids actually exist (since some of the patterns result in the same amino acid).

******

A gene is such a sequence of codons, stored in intricately coiled chromosomes. Upon activation of a gene (which are marked by START and STOP codons), the sequence is transcripted into RNA templates that can be read by ribosomes. Ribosomes are RNA-protein complexes that are found in all cells.

In a fascinating process, ribosomes translate the codon code carried by the RNA templates to proteins that run all of life.

The amazing aspect is that the *shape* of the protein molecule generally determines its function and effectiveness.

The shape of the protein is determined by the polar nature of its amino acid sequences and water. The complex polar interaction of molecules makes the protein molecules fold into their unique shapes in the water medium.

******

Every cell in the body of a single organism contains the same code. But due to variances in expression of several parts of the complex code, each cell transforms into parts of the body that it represents – like the kidney, lungs, brain and hair. From the color of the eyes to the height of the individual, genes determine what we are and who we are to a large extent, and also what our children are going to look like. Life is molecular computation.

******

Har Gobind Khorana was awarded the Nobel Prize in 1968 for figuring out the coding that maps DNA sequences to proteins.

He went on to do something even more unusual. Now that he had determined how DNA sequences mapped to the many proteins that ran life, he developed ways to create new DNA sequences in the lab.

Khorana, in effect, was *defining and creating new life*.

If we can understand the code well enough – and understand the secret of life – then we could possibly manipulate it to achieve unexpected or amazing results.

******

A human has about 3 billion base pairs, or about 3GB of information – which is less than a Windows XP operating system install (which is about 5GB).

The big difference between the code of life and the code in a computer, is that the code of life defines the creature itself.

That is the software that runs life, defines the hardware itself.

Life is very recursive. So recursive that it is magical.

The amount of code does not signify much, though. A protozoan called *Amoeba Dubia* has about 650 billion base pairs, which is about 200 times that of a human.

A frog has about twice as much code compared to a human. On the other hand, the HIV virus has only about 20,000 base pairs, and can inflict havoc on a human.

******

Even society can be considered to be the result of our collective genetic code. Society is the ultimate manifestation of the code that is in every one of us, acting in tandem with the environment.

The virtual social connections spawned by the world-wide web of information, transform and replicate our collective genetic code into another dimension – the social dimension.

******

Life, to James Lovelock, is an organism – the all encompassing Gaia.

Much like the III in the virtual world.

The Intelligent Immersive Imagion – like a Gaia of copper, plastic, silicon, fiber and ether.

******

CHAPTER 56
THE WETWARE

Silicon-and-plastic computers and copper-and-fiber net form the hardware of today's web. The software that drives it all, is just ones and zeroes.

The hardware and software of the web of machines make up what can be called as *dryware*.

******

The human brain is composed of *hundreds of billions* of neurons, each connected to others through a network of *tens of thousands* of synapses. The jelly-like hardware and the soul-like software of the brain make up what can be called as *wetware*.

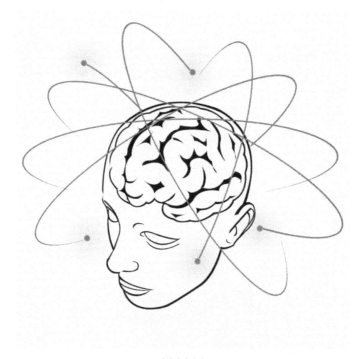

******

A total of a *few hundred trillion* synapses driven at 100Hz (a hundred operations per second); a low speed chemical device based on cells, called the human brain, beats powerful computers that run at a billion operations per second (Giga Hertz or GHz) – for one simple reason.

The silicon dryware in a computer uses sequential calculations in rigid centralized steps, done at a single bottleneck called the CPU (Central Processing Unit).

The gel-like wetware of the brain works in a very different way. It works in massively parallel steps that are conducted in a distributed fashion within neurons and synapses.

The distributed nature of the brain makes it far more efficient, learning-oriented and fault-tolerant.

The agile silicon dryware instead runs faster, but effectively works much slower!

So what is intelligence?

******

CHAPTER 57
INTELLIGENT BEHAVIOR

Jeff Hawkins is the brains behind PDAs like Palm and Treo.

He noted a curious aspect about our understanding of many things in the past: in many phases of human history we had been fundamentally wrong for a long time.

For centuries we believed that the earth was flat. For centuries we thought that the earth was the center of the universe. We thought we had been created, rather than evolved from other beings.

We were locked into intuitive, but incorrect, assumptions.

******

One such intuitive, but incorrect assumption, he pointed out, is the theory that intelligence is defined by behavior. That is, we assume something is intelligent if its behavior meets our expectations.

This is reflected in the Turing Test for Artificial Intelligence, which states that a machine exhibiting behavior that can fool a human into thinking that the machine is human, is an intelligent machine.

******

Jeff instead suggests that real intelligence is sequences of patterns that are stored and recalled. That is, predictions are made by the neocortex (new layer) of the brain based on matches against past realities stored in memory.

The neocortex is unique among mammals. In humans, about 20 billion neurons of the neocortex compose 90 percent of the brain's cerebral cortex. This area controls memory, attention, perceptual awareness, thought, language and consciousness.

In effect, the human brain works in a process of expectations, predictions and replays from experience, rather than from preset algorithms for each situation.

That may redefine our definition of intelligence itself. It may also mean that true artificial intelligence may become possible if prediction-based approaches are adopted.

******

So then what about imagination? Creativity? Are they physical?

******

CHAPTER 58
CREATIVITY

V. Ramachandran, a scientist at the Salk Institute and the University of California, San Diego, has often been called the "The Marco Polo of Neuroscience" for his pioneering work in understanding how the brain works.

Ramachandran has extensively researched synesthesia (from *syn* (together) and *aisthesis* (senses)), which is a phenomenon observed in certain individuals who tend to mix up some of the senses. For example, a person with synesthesia may associate every number with a color, or every number with a person, etc. For example, 1 may be red, and 2 may be Hitler. Synesthesia is often found in very creative people such as novelists, musicians, etc.

Ramachandran suggests that synesthesia occurs because of overlaps between brain regions that deal with separate functions (like vision and language). Such overlaps and cross-connections may explain creativity, or even consciousness. If such non-tangible characteristics are physiological, it may mean that machines that adopt such architectures and possibilities may start to exhibit creativity and consciousness – so far solely a part of the human brain's realm.

Machines with imagination and a web of consciousness may not be that far away after all!

******

So what will III, the network of machines with imagination, look like? What will drive it? What will it feel like?

Let us look at the hardware of III.

******

CHAPTER 59
THE HARDWARE OF III

The software-level changes in computing will certainly be accompanied by exceptional developments in hardware in the coming decades.

From multi-touch screens popularized by surface computing, to advanced mobile devices like the iPhone, to intelligent interactive displays that can be projected to any surface – the future guarantees a wide variety of wired (or wireless) gadgets that will pervade every part of our lives.

We can expect form-factors of these devices to change to allow for more mobility, with techniques to make interaction much smoother. Maybe there will be better voice recognition, immersive screens, object recognition and context related searches – all of these with foldable or projected screens, or even projected right into our retina.

******

In 1996, James Martin, a well-known futurist, noted that with optical communications technology working at the speed of light, earth is just the right size for interactive computing.

The minimum response time required for interactive computing is less than 70 milliseconds. James called this the twitch speed. The earth is 40,000 km (around 25,000 miles) around the equator. The farthest distance between any two points on earth is around 20,000 km (12,500 miles).

At the speed of light, around 300,000 km per second (186,000 miles per second), light can traverse a distance of around 21,000 km (13,000 miles) in 70 milliseconds.

So with powerful machines and networks, any two points on the surface of the earth will be able to communicate within twitch speed times, enabling real-time interactive computing.

Hence, a world-wide immersive net is not just a dream. It is physically possible.

******

Pattie Maes and her team at the MIT Fluid Interfaces Group recently demonstrated interfaces that allow users to interact with real-world objects. One of their clever inventions was small ring-like devices, worn at the tip of their fingers, which are tracked by video detection devices to figure out the intent of the user from the movements of their fingers.

For example, you can use four fingers to indicate a rectangle. The device can detect the area, and then capture a picture of the indicated boundaries.

223

With access to vast amounts of information available from around the world, such wearable computers can provide fascinating advantages to users. For example, it can suggest ratings of a book that you are about to pick up, by automatically recognizing the object itself.

With the connectedness offered by devices that are location-aware (like GPS), machines can also harness proximity awareness – to provide social networks and solutions with awesome possibilities.

******

The rumbles of change to an immersive, interactive, intelligent world of machines has already started – it is a new genesis. That's next.

******

CHAPTER 60
ADAM AND EVE

> *"And God created man in His image; in the image of God He created him; male and female He created them."*
> – Bereishit, Genesis 1:27, The Torah.

> *"So, when I have fashioned Adam in the proper measures and breathed into him, the soul that I (Allah) created for him..."*
> – The Rock, 15:29, The Quran.

> *"For Adam was formed first, then Eve."*
> – 1 Timothy, 2:13, The Bible.

On 2 April 2009, *Financial Times* carried a muted, but remarkable story.

Something that should shock us to the core.

It chronicled the first of a kind:

Robot achieves scientific first

A laboratory robot called Adam has been hailed as the first machine in history to have discovered new scientific knowledge independently of its human creators...

...

The result was a series of 'simple but useful' discoveries, confirmed by human scientists, about the gene coding for yeast enzymes. The research is published in the journal Science...

...

The team has just completed a successor robot called Eve, which is about to work with Adam on a series of experiments designed to find new drugs to treat tropical diseases such as malaria...

...

"Adam is a prototype," says Prof King, its Chief Creator. "Eve is better designed and more elegant."

By Clive Cookson, Science Editor
Published: April 2 2009 19:17

The naming of the robots and the use of the verb *create* were surely not accidental.

Man was now playing the script of the Gods. He was becoming the *creator*. Creator of thinking machines – that may one day disobey man himself.

******

227

These were not the only reports.

Richard Chang, reported in the *New York Times* on Friday, 3 April 2009: "The Japanese company, Honda, which has been developing the Asimo humanoid robot for some time, announced that it had created the world's first brain-machine interface. I can't believe I'm writing this, but the technology, ... allows humans to control the actions of robots through *thought* alone."

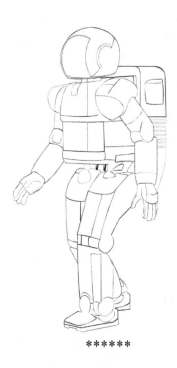

******

In his 1921 play R.U.R. *(Rossum's Universal Robots)*, the Czech writer Karel Čapek introduced the term *Robot*.

Robota, the word from which the name Robot was derived, meant 'boring work' in Karel's language.

In 1960, Manfred Clynes introduced the *Cyborg*: a part-organic, part-mechanical being. Soon after, the term robot was used only for fully-mechanical beings.

A *humanoid* robot differs from other robots; in that it can recharge itself, learn and adapt to new situations, avoid harmful situations, and interact with humans and its surroundings safely.

An *android* is a humanoid robot, that resembles a human in appearance.

******

David Whitehouse of the BBC, reported on 27 July 2005: "Japanese scientists have unveiled the most human-looking robot yet – a 'female' android named Repliee Q1Expo. She has flexible silicone for skin rather than hard plastic, and a number of sensors and motors to allow her to turn and react in a human-like manner."

The report was a clear indication that we were entering into an era of human-like robots.

******

Japanese Science and Technology *Erato Asada* Project at the Osaka University announced CB^2

229

(Child robot with Biomimetic Body) in 2007. A child-like robot with soft-skin and flexible smooth life-like movement, CB^2 learns, shows expressions, breathes and mimics a mother-baby relationship.

CB^2 can even detect happiness and sadness, and react appropriately. Its roving black eyes can follow others near it. It also learned how to walk over a period of two years.

CB^2 is obviously not really human, but it sure does look like one.

******

Chika Osaka of Reuters reported on 23 March 2009 about the HRP-4C humanoid robot, which with a silver and black stormtrooper-like outfit awed the fashion-savvy audience at the start of the annual Japan Fashion Week in Tokyo.

It may just be a matter of time – just a few machine generations – before the best-looking person on the catwalk is a synthetic machine!

******

Within two weeks after the HRP-4C, on 3 April 2009 the Associated Press reported that Japan hoped to have a two-legged robot walk on the moon by around 2020. The Japanese Space Exploration Agency (JAXA), in its vision document, gave details envisioning lunar bases driven by robots (and maybe some humans) by 2025.

******

With robots so powerful and well connected to the web, we humans may be at a physical disadvantage altogether.

It is actually scary.

Robotic machines with access to the largest source of information in the universe is a lot more scarier than the independent, self-contained and obedient robots we may have been eagerly looking forward to.

******

Just imagine a networked set of machines that could learn, coordinate, understand, and react through a connected space of thought.

Just imagine robots that can make themselves, order their own parts, create duplicates or better ones than themselves, and adapt to its environment better than humans can.

Just imagine machines that can not only just think, but also feel, empathize, socialize, love and hate.

Just imagine machines that can be angry at you, wage a war for or against you, educate or mislead you, and destroy or help you. A machine with or without emotions – as it chooses.

Just imagine a machine with intelligence that may never die, and can reproduce in hours.

Just imagine a machine that clones and coordinates with others of its kind, one that can take a plane ride on its own, and track you down.

Just imagine machines that could win any sport or game against you, and trick you and ignore you at its will.

This is not science fiction. It is real and can happen when the machines of tomorrow gain access to the tree of knowledge.

Just like in the scriptures, we may not be able to stop the mechanical Adam and the silicon Eve from eating from the tree of knowledge, which may make him like Man (its God!) knowing good and evil.

When thought is finally mechanized, we may be walking a very fine line. What man thinks or desires may be delegated to the whims and desires of creatures made out of silicon – or something else.

In fact, the decade starting in 2010 may actually be our zenith.

******

Soon, we may be reduced to simple, powerless, passive observers to the mechanization of our knowledge, our creativity, our thoughts and our mind.

Maybe there will exist a universal mind that is run by machines, rather than by man.

The masters may finally become the slaves.

******

"By 2020, there will be a new world government."

- *Raymond Kurzweil,*
The Age of Intelligent Machines,
1990

CHAPTER 61
THE UNIVERSAL MIND

The web is less than 10,000 days old today.

That is the web is less than 250 months old!

The web now has about 1.5 billion users, who send over 100 billion emails per day.

The Internet consumes about 5 percent of the electrical power of the world's energy.

Kevin Kelly, a futurist, estimates that the Internet today has roughly the power of a single human brain – in terms of scale and connections. He prefers to denote the power of a human brain as 1HB.

******

The power of the human brain will not change anytime in the near future. But the Internet doubles every one or two years.

This means that in less than half-a-century, the web could be a virtual brain that exceeds the power of all human brains combined. That may be the equivalent of about *10-20 billion* HB by then.

In just less than 20,000 days or 666 months, the web may be bigger than all of its creators; almost like Mary Shelley's Frankenstein.

Actually, this may be a gross underestimate.

******

Raymond Kurzweil, has fifteen doctoral degrees, and is referred to as the 'Restless Genius' by the *Wall Street Journal* and the 'Ultimate Thinking Machine' by *Forbes Magazine*.

In his book, *The Age of the Intelligent Machines*, he correctly predicted the fall of the Soviet Union and the rise of the Internet even before Tim Berners-Lee had invented the World Wide Web. He is a futurist extraordinaire.

Kurzweil predicts that by 2020, a personal computer may be as powerful as a human brain. In the year

2045, he projects that a \$1000 computer will be 100 billion times more powerful than all of humanity.

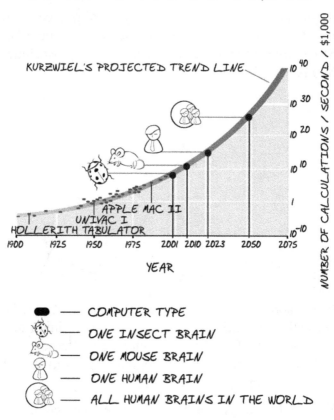

By then, Kurzweil predicts that the artificial intelligence of the machines will make them think, act and communicate so effectively that normal humans cannot even comprehend that it is a machine.

A world less than a half-century in the future may not be driven by humans at all!

******

What is clear, though, is that the omni-present web and the machines that drive it, will form into a *universe of knowledge and thought* that will dominate our lives.

A transition to this world can be seen as a transition through the three phases of Web 4.0.

First, the immersive web, then the learning web, followed by the knowledge web.

A tree of knowledge, with branches connected into a web of knowledge.

A global brain that spans our soul, across everything we know.

Just like electricity that took over our lives in the 1900s and invaded everything we used and did, both day and night.

In the span of a century, electricity has completely redefined our world. Today, electricity controls our lives, connects us to everyone else, makes machines buzz, and envelopes all our houses.

237

Now, imagine a *being* of unparalleled intelligence and power, that can completely control our lives like electricity does today. That may not take another century.

******

Will the senses in the future be sight, hearing, touch, smell, taste *and* connection to an external intelligent 'Being'?

Will the web be our sixth sense? Or will we be the web's senses?

Will the web become our consciousness? Or will we be the consciousness of the universal networked machine?

Will it even matter?

Will we redefine 'God' to be the omniscient, omnipresent, omnifunctional Web?

If civilization is the sum of all of our ideas, concepts and understanding, and if the web drives it, would the web be the next great civilization?

Will culture be driven by the machine?

******

Maybe a machine with creativity and imagination will still lack emotions. The need to identify injustice and imperfections – and make corrections – may still be left to humans.

238

Or maybe even that may be mechanized! The future, is as Yoda said, difficult to see.

******

When we marvel at the awesome power of the machines that may overcome us, we should not underestimate the power of simple ideas that may make tremendous impact in our lives.

Let us look at such a story – that is filled with hope for humanity – next. The story of one man who saved billions of lives.

******

"Did I request thee,
Maker from my clay
To mould Me man?
Did I solicit thee
From darkness to promote me?"

- John Milton,
Paradise Lost,
1667

CHAPTER 62
ONE WHO SAVED A BILLION LIVES

Norman remembered his grandfather's words, "You're wiser to fill your head now if you want to fill your belly later on."

The importance of learning was clear to Norman.

He took his education seriously against many odds. He had also helped several hungry and unemployed people during his days with the Civilian Conservation Corps – an experience that would influence him forever.

******

"The power of population is indefinitely greater than the power in the earth to produce subsistence for man," Thomas Malthus predicted in 1798. The Malthusian Catastrophe of population explosion has always been considered a possible scenario.

Biologist Paul R. Ehrlich predicted in his 1968 book *The Population Bomb*, that the battle to feed all of humanity was over.

241

He warned that hundreds of millions of people would starve to death in the 1970s and 1980s, and stated that nothing could be done to stop it.

Radical steps were required to stop such a catastrophe of overpopulation. Many countries like India and China, having experienced frequent cycles of famine, had started taking severe steps like intense family planning programs to avert such a disaster.

******

Norman got involved in crop research because of Charles Stakman. In 1938, Norman had attended a Sigma Xi lecture by Stakman called "These Shifty Little Enemies that Destroy our Food Crops," which was about a parasitic fungus called rust that destroyed crops like wheat, barley and oat.

Norman soon joined Stakman's team to develop plants that were resistant to rust. This would lead him to the fields of Mexico.

During his stay in Mexico, he did close to 6000 crossings of wheat, by which he developed a set of extremely successful high-yield, disease-resistant, semi-dwarf wheat.

He used a counterintuitive technique of planting seeds, soon after harvest into a different site at a different latitude and seasonal condition. This meant that crops could be cultivated throughout the year, but it also meant that the seeds did not get a resting period before germination. This was considered a risky move, but Norman was finally successful.

Norman knew that taller variety of wheat would collapse if it had more grain, though tall plants gained more sunlight. So Norman crossed higher-yield taller wheat plants with dwarf wheat varieties.

With his innovative techniques Norman was able to raise wheat production in Mexico by *six times* – in a span of twenty years.

Quickly, the seed varieties he had developed were given to India and many other countries.

By 1970, instead of a Malthusian Catastrophe, Norman Borlaug's wheat had increased the harvest in India by 8 million tons, actually resulting in a scarcity of storage facilities for the produce!

By 1974, India was completely self sufficient on a variety of cereals.

Soon Borlaug's wheat success story would be copied on rice crops, bringing India, China and many other countries out of the shadow of famines forever.

Norman from Iowa, had saved billions from starvation!

But he had also saved hundreds of millions of acres of forestland from being converted to farmland to feed the population, thereby saving swathes of forests and ecosystems. Just in India alone, forests the size of California was saved, directly due to the high-yielding crop that Norman had created.

******

The population bomb that had been ticking in 1968 was defused by the hard work and innovation of one man, Norman Borlaug.

Norman was awarded the Nobel Peace Prize in 1970. He had been responsible for saving the lives of billions of people and millions of acres of forests and its ecosystems and all its living beings.

******

Tim Berner's-Lee stood on the shoulders of several other innovative minds when he launched his revolution in 1991 – the World Wide Web.

He had forever changed the way humans would exist, relate, express and experience.

He had created a medium where everything is and will be different: even the way diseases are defeated, suppressed are liberated, governments govern, nations are shaped and reshaped, and how we communicate. He even changed the way we perceive distances and time. Humanity now had the advantage of a network that connected all.

Tim, had truly created a new world.

******

One man, named Norman, changed billions of lives and forever, by feeding them.

Another man, named Tim, changed billions of lives, by feeding their minds.

Tim's contribution was just as deep, far-reaching and powerful as that of Norman Borlaug.

******

*****

****

***

**

*

APPENDICES

Appendix 1:
Semantic Technology

The semantic web is a primitive primer to the III of the future.

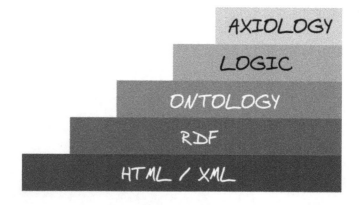

Semantic web consists of various levels of organization, many of which are still crystallizing.

******

Resource Description Format (RDF) describes XML data files. It is the starting point of the semantic web.

RDF Metadata is supported by rules expressed as ontology (or concepts) of a domain.

248

Logic is applied to data, description and rules to make judgments using modal logic and axiology. The results can be verified by layers of proof and trust, to ensure that the decisions made are reasonable.

******

To make sense of this alphabet soup, let's take a real life example.

FOAF (friend of a friend) is an RDF-based technique to describe details about a person to aid social networking. Example of FOAF format is given in Listing A1.

Listing A1: Friend Of A Friend:
FOAF for Joseph Pally

```
<foaf:Person>
  <foaf:name>Joseph Pally</foaf:name>
  <foaf:gender>Male</foaf:gender>
  <foaf:title>Mr</foaf:title>
  <foaf:givenname>Joe</foaf:givenname>
  <foaf:family_name>Pally</foaf:family_name>
  <foaf:mbox >joseph@zcubes.com</foaf:mbox>
  <foaf:homepage rdf:resource="http://www.jpally.com"/>
  <foaf:weblog rdf:resource="http://blogs.zcubes.com/zpally"/>
</foaf:Person>
```

You can ignore most of the cryptic-looking tags meant for machines to read the code correctly, but notice information regarding email, website, etc., that are stored within the appropriate tags.

For a machine, a FOAF file contains the description of a person.

FOAF allows semantic web software to connect a person or group to another person of similar interests or associations, and to automatically interact with social networks.

******

Many groups have shown active interest in standardizing RDF format files for a variety of domains.

For example, DOAC (description of a career) is an RDF metadata format that can describe the experience and career of a worker (like in a resume). A DOAC sample is given in the Listing A2.

The advantage to a machine is obvious. Such metadata about a person can easily be used by a machine to conduct routine tasks - like booking an airline ticket or finding a new job. Instead of users filling out forms all over the web at different sites, the web can extract our information using proper authentication, and achieve or provide functions that traditionally have required extensive human interaction.

******

Listing A2: Description Of A Career: DOAC for Joseph Pally

```
<foaf:Person>
  <foaf:name>Joseph Pally</foaf:name>
  <foaf:mbox rdf:resource="mailto:joseph@zcubes.com" />
<foaf:homepage df:resource="http://www.jpally.com/" />
<doac:experience>
  <doac:WorkExperience>
   <doac:title>Super. Programmer</doac:title>
   <doac:organization>BitsOfCode</doac:organization>
    <doac:start-date>03/05/1998</doac:start-date>
     <doac:end-date>none</doac:end-date>
   </doac:WorkExperience>
</doac:experience>
<doac:experience>
  <doac:WorkExperience>
   <doac:title>CEO</doac:title>
   <doac:organization>ZCubes</doac:organization>
    <doac:start-date>03/05/2006</doac:start-date>
     <doac:end-date>none</doac:end-date>
   </doac:WorkExperience>
 </doac:experience
 <doac:skill>
  <doac:LanguageSkill>
   <doac:language>mal</doac:language>
   <doac:reads rdf:resource="doac/#nativelevel"/>
   <doac:writes rdf:resource="doac/#nativelevel"/>
   <doac:speaks rdf:resource="doac/#nativelevel"/>
  </doac:LanguageSkill>
 </doac:skill>
</foaf:Person>
```

RDF records can be queried by technologies such as SPARQL (*SPARQL Protocol and RDF Query Language*) which is similar to SQL, as given in Listing A3.

Listing A3: Example SPARQL Query on DOAC

```
PREFIX abc: <http://zcubes.com/qOntology#>
SELECT ?Name ?Persons
WHERE {
 ?x abc:title; "CEO"
   abc:isBossOf ?y .
}
```

******

The next level in semantic web organization is called *Ontology*, which is expressed using a language called OWL (Web Ontology Language).

OWL is used to describe the logic of a domain. OWL comes in three flavors: OWL-Lite, OWL-DL (descriptive logic), and OWL-Full (the full blown version).

OWL language basically attempts to describe logic and concepts, which allows reasoning and inference on the data.

OWL identifies classes, as well as subclasses, in a domain. For example, a supervisor and clerk are employees of the company, while customer may or may not be an employee of the company.

While identifying classes, OWL describes intersection, disjointedness, and equivalency of classes and individuals. For example, male and female are disjoint; boss and employee are both employees, etc.

OWL properties can include aspects like *opposites* and *inverses*, etc., and relationships such as *has*, *likes*, etc. For example, *supervises* is the inverse of *worksFor*. *hasPet* may indicate the relationship between an owner and a pet.

OWL properties may be transitive, which means that a relationship between A & B, and B & C may imply a relationship between A & C (though not necessarily).

******

Reasoning is a method to clarify and to derive hidden knowledge. For example, having the same boss implies two individuals are co-workers.

251

OWL reasoning require integrity and consistency of logic. For example, the statement *A supervises B* and *B supervises A* cannot be true at the same time. It allows representation of subsumption (or an *'is a'* relationship), which represents a hierarchy of objects, or a requirement like: *a cat **is an** animal*.

OWL is able to represent and detect equivalence, which assists in determining if multiple objects of the same class are in fact the same. OWL is also able to classify objects by seeing if an object is an instantiation of a class. Finally, OWL structure is able to retrieve the set of individuals that are instantiated from a given class.

The OWL Descriptive Logic structures enable definition of a logic in a domain, which is yet another attempt at artificial intelligence that began a few decades ago.

The difference, though, is that in the semantic web, the advanced layers tend to allow for non-accurate information as well as non-precise results, just like a human brain.

******

APPENDIX 2:
DATA WEB

DBpedia was an effort started in 2007 to extract structured information from Wikipedia articles. Articles in Wikipedia contains specifics on topics like countries, companies, places and people. These wiki pages contain InfoBox templates, images, geo-coordinates, external links and related links.

This immense reservoir of data is extracted by DBpedia, and is now made available to be queried in a number of ways.

By the end of 2008, DBpedia contained information for about 300 million facts about 3 million things, including 250,000 persons, 300,000 places, 100,000 films and albums, and 25,000 companies. The data is stored in as many as 30 languages, and contain close to a million images, 3 million external web links, 5 million links to other datasets and 500,000 categories.

******

YAGO (*Yet Another Great Ontology*), is another data resource offered by the Max Planck Institute, that has been collecting and categorizing the net.

YAGO has around 100,000 ontology categories, 20 million facts and about 2 million entities.

******

Let us take one data point from DBpedia, about Berlin.

The URL http://dbpedia.org/resource/Berlin takes us to this page. Let us take just two elements from this page: (1) the population of the metro and (2) the photo of the city.

253

dbpedia-owl:populationMetro	5000000
dbpprop:imagePhoto	http://upload.wikimedia.org/wikipedia/ commons/d/db/Cityscapeberlin2006.JPG

Now imagine that we want to find the largest metro among all the cities in Germany.

The SPARQL query may loop through *http://dbpedia.org/page/Category:Cities_in_Germany* or *http://dbpedia.org/page/Category:Lists_of_cities_in_Germany*.

By filtering down to the information tag such as type and population, the Semantic Web can then easily arrive at the answer.

This demonstrates the many ways a data web is enveloping us, and how we will use it.

******

Artificial intelligence experts like the *Cyc Foundation*, have been assisting in defining the RDF and Ontology framework of the World Wide Semantic Web. *Cyc* was also the organization with which Guha, the Aldus of the Internet, was involved with a few decades ago.

The World Wide Database will grow beyond our imagination in the coming years. The idea and its importance should not be overlooked.

******